DATE DUE

DEC 2 8 2011		
JAN 1 3 2012		
JAN 3 1 2012		
MAR 0 6 2012		
MAR 2 0 2012		
APR 2 0 2012		
MAY 1 7 2012		

P9-CIV-003

SCORPIONS *for* BREAKFAST

SCORPIONS
for
BREAKFAST

My Fight Against Special Interests,
Liberal Media, and Cynical Politicos to
Secure America's Border

Governor Jan Brewer

BROADSIDE BOOKS
An Imprint of HarperCollins*Publishers*
www.broadsidebooks.net

HarperCollins books may be purchased for educational, business, or sales
promotional use. For information, please write: Special Markets Department, HarperCollins Publishers, 10 East 53rd Street, New York, NY 10022.

Broadside Books™ and the Broadside logo are trademarks of HarperCollins
Publishers.

FIRST EDITION

Library of Congress Cataloging-in-Publication

Scorpions for breakfast : my fight against special interests, liberal media,
and cynical politicos to secure America's border / by Jan Brewer.—1st ed.

p.   cm.

ISBN: 978-0-06-210639-1

1. Border security—United States. I. Title.

JV6483.B73   2011

363.28'50973—dc23   2011032469

11 12 13 14 15   OV/RRD   10 9 8 7 6 5 4 3 2 1

To those who've shared this journey with me:
John, Ronald, John, and Michael

CONTENTS

Foreword

by Governor Sarah Palin

For weeks, April 24, 2010, had been circled on my calendar. With my Alaska home still surrounded by snow, I looked forward to traveling "outside" America's forty-ninth state to the forty-eighth, where spring had already sprung.

I was scheduled to give a speech about "challenges and overcoming adversity" in Glendale, while the eyes of the nation were fixed on the rough-and-tumble debate over the Grand Canyon State's immigration policy. It was on April 23, the day before my speech, that Arizona governor Jan Brewer put pen to paper and sent a ringing wake-up call to the White House and the federal government with a legislative message that would change the country.

She had signed SB 1070 into law.

It was during this breathless political drama that I met Jan for the first time. I was immediately struck by her determination, her kindness and concern, and her good spirit, and sensed that in the face of an international media firestorm, Jan Brewer was still a down-to-earth mom committed to public service and principled leadership.

In my speech in Glendale I publicly thanked Jan for her courage, and have followed her progress and success carefully since then. As we've experienced the uniqueness of each other's states together, I've gotten to know her better.

Like many of us, she was called to public life after first getting involved with the education of her children. I'm never surprised when I hear that a stint with the PTA or local school board helped bring someone into even more robust public service. School boards just seem to get the political blood pumping in mama grizzlies.

Jan has risen from local government to the governor's office. And she's done it by bringing people together—by building up, instead of tearing down. Her strong conservative values are matched by a driving optimism that seems to know no end. Above all else, Jan Brewer is an authentic leader. She talks straight and does what she believes is right for the people she serves—even when it's the hard thing to do.

As you'll see in this book, Jan doesn't back down from tough challenges. She doesn't turn away in the face of attacks. She leans into problems and works toward meaningful, achievable solutions.

Arizonans are lucky to have Jan Brewer on their side. And our country is a better place because of her honest, humble commitment to everlasting American freedom.

I'm thankful she's leading and I'm proud to call her a friend.

—Sarah Palin, summer 2011

SCORPIONS *for* BREAKFAST

INTRODUCTION: WATERBOARDED

The best comparison I could think of was: This must be what it's like to be waterboarded.

There I was, in my office at the Arizona Capitol, with a bill about which everyone in America seemed to have an opinion—and a strong one at that. Advice, objections, encouragement, discouragement, fan letters, and death threats were coming at me so fast I could barely breathe. And not just me but my staff, the Arizona legislators who had worked on the bill—all of us felt as if we were strapped to a board with torrents of accusations raining down on our heads. Manning the buckets were the national media, the unions, civil rights groups, business groups, and political operatives all the way up to the president himself. Was it torture? I never did ask Dick Cheney, but I'll tell you this: It was not an experience I want to repeat.

It was a surreal time to be the governor of the Grand Canyon State. For weeks, protesters had been massing outside my windows on the ninth floor of the executive tower of the Capitol. They were there every day, marching, chanting, and beating drums. Always beating drums. Some of them flew Mexican flags. Some of them desecrated American flags. Our supporters were there, too, of course, but they were a lower-key bunch. They tended to sing the national anthem rather than chant, and to quote the U.S. Constitution rather than Che Guevara. Things eventually got so testy between the two sides that the peace officers had to form a human chain between the supporters and the protesters. It was an amazing scene. The chanting. The drumming. The Constitution quoting. Only in America.

The reason for all this passion was Senate Bill 1070, the now famous law that I signed as a tool to help secure our southern border. You may think you know something about what was quickly dubbed America's "toughest immigration law," but chances are, if you're a devoted consumer of MSNBC and the *New York Times*, you don't know much at all about our law. Its opponents call it racist. The Obama administration calls it unconstitutional. Supporters call it necessary. I call it a wake-up call. I signed it to send a clear, unequivocal message to Washington. It's a message that I've repeated more times than I care to count during my three years as Arizona's governor. It's a message that's long past due. And it's a message that Washington very clearly doesn't want to hear:

Mr. President: Do your job. Secure our border!

That's it—simple and direct. Kind of like me. Kind of like Arizona.

The story of the Support Our Law Enforcement and Safe Neighborhoods Act, or SB 1070, is a story of a state in crisis. That state is my state, Arizona. We're dealing with a crisis caused by drug dealers, human smugglers, generic criminals, and the sheer volume of people pouring over our unsecured border. Innocents are being victimized. People are living in fear. Our beautiful desert is being ruined. The story of SB 1070 is a story of leadership—and its opposite. It's the story of how the people of the state of Arizona took charge of their own future after decades of benign neglect and not-so-benign indifference from Washington. It's the story of how Arizonans stepped up to lead when their representatives in Washington failed to do so. The citizens of Arizona didn't want this fight. They didn't cause this crisis. But they're not going to sit still anymore. Not when they can do something about it.

The story of SB 1070 is also the story of a country—a great country—whose ending is yet to be written. Immigration has made America great. *Illegal* immigration threatens to fundamentally change our country, and not in a way that the Norwegians, Poles, Italians, Jews, Irish, Chinese, Kenyans, Cubans, Mexicans, and others who waited their turn in line to come here legally would approve of. They all came because here the law was supreme. Here the law meant something. It ensured a level playing field. It made sure that everyone got an equal chance—and if they didn't, the law had something to say about it. They came here and embraced a set of values that made them Americans.

But in the end, the story of SB 1070 is the story of an arrogant, out-of-control federal government. The people of Arizona watched for years as our border went unenforced, as our schools and hospitals became overwhelmed with poor, desperate illegal aliens, and, finally, as violent crime invaded our cities when the Mexican drug cartels took over the border crossings. We saw all this happening and we appealed to our federal government for help. We asked them to do their job. And when they refused, we acted. We passed a law to protect ourselves because the federal government wouldn't. And what did we get for our effort? We were demonized and called racists. We were sued and treated like subjects instead of citizens. We were told that the federal government will enforce the law how it chooses and when it chooses. We were slapped down like wayward children.

The level of illegal immigration across the southwestern border is not what it was in the years and months leading up to my signing of SB 1070. The recession has eliminated many of the jobs that illegal aliens once came to this country to take. But there is no reason to believe that once the economy improves, we won't return to the 1,000-a-day illegal crossings that we saw at the height of the crisis. There has been no fundamental change in Mexico that would cause Mexican citizens to want to stay. Mexican economic policy is still broken, many of their officials are still corrupt, and cartel violence is still at an all-time high.

Another reason I believe that border crossings are down is because we've proved that enforcing the law works. Speaking for Arizona, the tough laws we've implemented (or tried to implement in the case of SB 1070) have had an effect. As we'll see, SB 1070 was just the latest in a string of Arizona actions—actions like enforcing the law against employing illegal aliens, ensuring the integrity of our elections by requiring proof of citizenship, and limiting most state services to legal residents. These efforts, I believe, are beginning to have the damping effect on illegal immigration that they were intended to have. Fewer people are willing to take the risk of coming to a state that takes its laws seriously.

We don't really know the cause—or the causes—of the reported decrease in illegal border crossings. But this we do know: The reports of the death of the crisis of illegal immigration are, to borrow a phrase, greatly exaggerated. Even though the apprehensions of illegals at the border have declined, the number of illegal aliens in the United States was unchanged between 2009 and 2010. That's because 45 percent of illegal aliens in the United States are people who have overstayed their visas. The federal government reports that about 200,000 people overstayed their visas in 2009. Of these, fewer than 2,000—or less than 1 percent—were tracked down and deported. And yet, while visa overstaying accounts for almost half of the illegal aliens in the United States, the rejection rates for Mexicans seeking tourist visas have reportedly fallen from 32 percent to 11 percent under the Obama administration. Who knew all the people sneaking across our border just wanted to visit the Grand Canyon and see the sights! While the Obama administration seems determined to make the problem worse, laws like Arizona's SB 1070 are designed to address visa overstayers by enforcing the law against people being here illegally once they have already crossed the border.

While the politicians who fly over the border occasionally in helicopters may think the immigration crisis is over, those who live and work down on the border know otherwise. We live this issue every day. Arizonans who live next door to a drop house, whose homes have been broken into, who've hiked through the desert and seen the mountains of trash left by illegal crossers . . . well, their view is different from the one in Washington, D.C.

Illegal immigration in America today mocks the law, much the same way our president mocks those he disagrees with on the issue. President Obama has repeatedly made fun of those of us who want to see the law enforced, saying we want a "moat" with "alligators" in it around our country. The reason he has resorted to these failed attempts at humor, I think, is that he supports a policy that is fundamentally undemocratic, and he knows it. Whether it's a so-called sanctuary city or the federal government suing Arizona for trying to enforce federal law, by selectively choosing which laws to enforce, the federal government damages all of our laws. It thereby damages democracy itself. If our representatives pass laws that can then be ignored by our government, what control do we have over our destinies? How can we call ourselves a free and self-governing people?

My own role in this story has been dictated by something my mother once told me: Doing the right thing almost always means doing the hard thing. This battle has been hard, but it has also been right. At the time I signed SB 1070, I didn't realize the overwhelming impact it would have on the national level. I saw a problem, and I saw a solution. I didn't appreciate how threatening that solution would be to some people. I've always been idealistic about Americans, and especially Arizonans. That idealism has never failed me. I live in the best state in the greatest country in the world. I thought that if I was conscientious and had the people with me, I could expect those who call themselves our leaders to give me a fair hearing. I thought that by doing the right thing, I could avoid being called a bad person. I thought that by proposing practical solutions, I could cut through the politics.

I was wrong.

I am not the first governor to find herself in a no-holds-barred, take-no-prisoners battle with Washington and the liberal media. But in Arizona, our fight is different, and all the more frustrating for it. While most reform-minded governors fight Washington for the freedom to do their jobs without federal micromanagement, I am fighting Washington to make it get off its keister and do what it's supposed to do.

The Constitution is very clear on this point. We looked it up.

Article IV, Section 4 imposes on the federal government the duty to "protect each [state] against Invasion and . . . . domestic Violence." I don't want anything more controversial than for Barack Obama to honor these words. I don't want anything more radical than for the law to be enforced.

And yet there I was, being called names you would never want your children and grandchildren to hear. I was called "Hitler's daughter." I was called "Satan's whore." Mostly, I was called things I can't repeat here. Why? When did enforcing the law become controversial? The sheer volume and hysteria of the reaction we had provoked made me think that we were on to something. During World War II, my father worked at the U.S. Naval Ammunition Depot in Hawthorne, Nevada, the biggest ammunition depot in the world at that time. He supervised the men who packed the explosives into the casings to make the bombs used in Germany and Japan. The pilots who delivered these bombs had a saying: "If you're not catching flak, you're not over the target." I thought of that as the howls of protest rose over Arizona's immigration law. We must have been over a very important target, because we were catching a heck of a lot of flak.

My fellow governor over in New Jersey, the incomparable Chris Christie, has made himself a YouTube sensation by turning the flak coming at him into bunker-busting rhetorical missiles aimed back at his opponents. And Scott Walker, my Republican colleague up in Wisconsin, has taken his share of incoming and not only survived but lived to claim victory. There are other examples of leaders more visionary and more courageous than me who have found themselves receiving the wrath of the Washington establishment.

Christie felt the heat for taking on the powerful, too often corrupt, status quo in New Jersey that had driven his state off a fiscal cliff. Walker felt it for challenging the powerful, arrogant public sector unions that had done the same. In Arizona, we were punished for taking on the granddaddy of them all, the all-powerful federal government. We had the gumption—call it the *audacity*—to demand that Washington do its job and secure our national border. That in itself isn't very audacious, of course, unless it turns out that the federal government isn't interested in doing its job—that it has *no intention* of doing its job.

That, in a nutshell, is what is happening in Arizona today: The people have risen up and demanded that Washington do a job it has no intention of doing. Call us yokels, call us rednecks, but we take our laws seriously in Arizona. One would think Congress would do the same.

To be fair, the failure to secure our border has been a bipartisan problem in America for decades now. Both Republicans and Democrats can be faulted for not taking our border security seriously and leaving the states, also headed by Republicans and Democrats, feeling the pain. But today we have a government that has taken non-enforcement to the level of policy.

Politics, ideology, and special interests are some of the reasons why Washington doesn't want to secure the border. I'll go into all of them in this book. But in the end, the real obstacle is arrogance. It takes a pretty arrogant government to take a law that Congress has passed and simply refuse to enforce it—and to seek to prevent others from doing so. And this arrogance about illegal immigration is part and parcel of government arrogance in general. Government that wants to spend beyond its means and take over our health care decisions is government that has a different vision from what most Arizonans and, I would argue, most Americans would agree with. In Arizona, we fought back against that kind of arrogance. We haven't been willing to give up on our vision of America as a people that has a government, as Ronald Reagan used to say, not a government that has a people. We fought back and we got hammered for it. But in the end, the people have always been with us. They've always understood. I am more grateful for their support and encouragement than I can say.

Amid all the chaos, a group of people I don't even know started a Web site to defend me against all the obnoxious, hurtful accusations being recklessly thrown around. It was a tongue-in-cheek site in which people could post colorful descriptions of me. The actor and activist Chuck Norris alerted me to one of his favorites: Jan Brewer eats scorpions for breakfast.

I guess it was meant to be flattering. I guess it was meant to portray me as tough. But even if you're tough enough to start your day with a meal of deadly poisonous insects, it's not something you particularly want to do. You don't seek it out. You do it because there's no other honorable option.

It was late at night—past 11:00 P.M.—when Agent Brian Terry and his elite unit of the U.S. Border Patrol came upon a pack of heavily armed men last December. They were in Peck Canyon, about ten miles north of Nogales and the border. Terry and his unit were on the hunt for "rip crews"—gangs of criminals, often illegal aliens, who prey on the drug and human smugglers who inhabit the canyons of the desert Southwest. It was dark. A gun battle erupted. When the shooting stopped, Agent Terry was dead, shot in the back by a semiautomatic rifle.

For Arizonans, Agent Terry's death was one more tragic reminder of the reality we deal with every day. It came at the end of a year spent battling the federal government to do something about the violence on the border. Long used to negligence from Washington when it came to securing the border, we were now encountering resistance to our efforts to do something about it. Agent Terry's death, we thought, was the tragic outcome.

So imagine our shock and horror when we learned, seven months later, that not just federal negligence had contributed to Agent Terry's death, but, it seemed, federal *complicity* as well. It was revealed that weapons found at the scene of Agent Terry's killing had come from a program begun in November 2009 by the Obama Justice Department. Operation Fast and Furious was an operation of the Bureau of Alcohol, Tobacco and Firearms (ATF) to track weapons trafficking into Mexico. The ATF, with the backing of U.S. Attorney Dennis Burke, allowed more than 2,000 firearms to be purchased at Phoenix-area stores. The idea was for the ATF to track the weapons to the Mexican drug cartels, but they quickly lost track of the guns. Of the 2,020 firearms put into circulation during the operation, more than 1,400 remain on the street, in either Mexico or the United States. Two were found at the scene of the Peck Canyon shoot-out. The FBI has been unable to rule out the possibility that one of these guns was used to kill Agent Terry.

The news that the federal government may have, through its incompetence, been complicit in the killing of a Border Patrol agent was almost more than I could bear. I had had an exhausting year. The Obama administration had resisted my attempts to protect the people of my state with everything they had. We had been told that our efforts were racist. What's more, they said, our law would impede rather than assist law enforcement. But what was the federal government's idea of effective law enforcement? Allowing more than 2,000 weapons to "walk" across the border to criminals in Mexico. The unbridled arrogance of it was astonishing to me. The feds had told us that they knew best, and their "best" had helped get Agent Brian Terry killed. This is what it has come to, I thought. This is what Arizonans can expect from their federal government.

Six weeks earlier, I had been elected to a second term as Arizona's governor. It had been an eventful race, to say the least. I had been handed the reins of government in the midst of the worst financial crisis in Arizona's history. I had signed the most controversial law in anyone's memory. The Arizona attorney general, who was supposed to defend that law in court, had decided to run against me—all the while insisting that he could continue to defend it.

In the end, I was blessed to receive a wonderful mandate from the people of Arizona. But I knew it wasn't just *my* victory. Something bigger—much bigger—was happening. Standing on the podium on election night before a crowd of boisterous supporters, I knew this wasn't about me. It was about America. At first I decided to have a little fun with it.

"Tonight we foreclosed on a house—the one that used to be run by Nancy Pelosi!"

The crowd erupted in cheers.

Then I got serious.

"Here in Arizona, we have not forgotten what our state and our nation are made of," I said, my voice almost breaking with the emotion that I felt.

"We know what we are and we know what we are not. We

are a free and striving people who trust and care for each other. We are not the subjects of an arrogant and overbearing government."

A free and striving people. That's who we are. And that's who I am fighting to let us remain.

CHAPTER ONE

Crisis

When the sheriff's deputies finally found Rob Krentz, his dog, Blue, was still clinging to life. Even after fourteen hours lying, wounded, in the back of Rob's four-wheeler, Blue still fought to defend his master. But Blue's loyalty was for nothing. Rob was dead. They found him lying beside his still-idling vehicle, with a gunshot wound in his left side. The sheriff's office later said it had killed him within minutes.

As investigators pieced together the events that led up to Rob's death, we learned that the day Rob died, March 27, 2010, had been a pretty typical one. It began with him out on his four-wheeler, Blue by his side, working his sprawling 35,000-acre ranch in Cochise County, about twelve miles from the Mexican border. Rob was the third generation of the Krentz family to run the ranch, and it was more than a job. The land was both his livelihood and his life. And life in the desert Southwest is water. So Rob was out that morning checking the lines that delivered water to his 1,000 head of cattle.

If the day was a typical one, the last words Rob spoke to his brother Phil were also pretty unremarkable. At about 10:00 A.M., Rob radioed to say that he had found an illegal alien on his property. He was going to help him, Rob said, and Phil should contact the Border Patrol.

Like all the ranchers along the border, Rob regularly encountered exhausted, lost, and dehydrated illegal aliens on this land.

He was well known for helping these desperate souls with some water, some food, and a kind word or two in Spanish. He helped them despite the trash and the fires they left on his property, the cut fences and broken water lines, and the frightened, unsettled cattle. Rob once estimated that over a five-year period, illegal immigration through his ranch had cost him a whopping $8 million. The damage he suffered because of the unsecured border to his south was real. But Rob never lost his humanity. He was that kind of guy.

The Krentz family is an Arizona ranching institution. They have been ranching along the border since 1907. Rob worked the land along with Phil, Phil's son Ben, Rob's wife, Sue, and their son Frank, one of three children they had raised on the ranch. Rob had been outspoken about the threat illegal immigration posed to him and his neighbors. Their house had been broken into, they'd been physically threatened, and one of their calves had been butchered. But his was always the voice of reason, not hatred and resentment. He and Sue had repeatedly called on the federal government to do its job. That's all: just do its job and keep them safe.

As Phil Krentz hung up the radio that day, a seed of worry began to grow in his mind. The day before, Phil had spotted marijuana smugglers on the ranch and called the Border Patrol. Border agents responded and seized more than 200 pounds of marijuana and arrested eight illegal aliens. Phil knew that the Mexican drug cartels viciously guarded their smuggling routes. Was a member of the smuggling ring planning to take revenge on the Krentz family? Was Rob just in the wrong place at the wrong time? Had he seen too much?

Rob and Phil were supposed to meet up that day at noon. When Rob didn't show and didn't respond to Phil's radio calls, the Krentz family and friends took off on their ATVs to search the ranch. When they hadn't found Rob by six o'clock that evening, they made two calls: One was to Rob's wife, Sue, who was in Phoenix visiting family. Come home, they said. We can't find Rob. The second was to Cochise County sheriff Larry Dever. Sheriff Dever immediately contacted his search-and-rescue squad, and the Border Patrol responded as well. But it was after dark when the Arizona Department of Public Safety helicopter finally spotted Rob by the lights of his still-running ATV.

I was at home when I got the call. It was late at night. A highly regarded rancher had been killed in the south of the state, I was told. Rob Krentz had been killed. That's all they knew. I hung up the phone. And as I waited for my staff to get back to me with more information, I grieved, I worried, and I wondered. Everyone in Arizona, it seemed, either knew Rob or knew of him. I had met him at a couple of meetings with the ranchers. Had he been a victim of the escalating violence on the border? As I waited, I couldn't help but fear the worst. *Oh my God, what has happened? We have to get a handle on this.*

I was determined to find out exactly what had happened. I called Sheriff Dever. My staff kept me updated with any news. Soon we learned that the officers who responded to the scene had found some important clues. Whoever shot Rob had done so without warning: Rob's rifle and a pistol were found secured in his ATV. Still, Rob had managed to drive about 300 yards after he had been shot. By following the tracks of his four-wheeler, law enforcement found three spent bullet shells, and something else: the dusty footprints of one person. Trackers followed the footprints south for about twenty miles, all the way to the U.S.-Mexico border. Then they lost them. And that's where the trail went cold.

To this day, Rob Krentz's killer has never been found. Still, it's difficult to overstate the impact his death had on Arizona, and on America. After Rob was murdered, politicians from Representative Gabrielle Giffords to Senator John McCain joined me in calling for President Obama and Homeland Security Secretary Napolitano to deploy the National Guard to the border. Former congressman J. D. Hayworth, who was challenging Senator John McCain in the GOP primary at the time, called Rob a "martyr" for the cause of border security. Rob's funeral mass in Douglas attracted more than 1,000 people.

Many liberal critics in the mainstream media have attributed the passage of SB 1070 to the "hysterical" reaction to Rob's death. The fact is, the legislation had been working its way through the legislature for months before he was killed. But Rob's death gave the bill momentum. It's not as if people didn't see the killing coming. And it's not as if government was powerless to prevent it. After Rob was murdered, the idea of doing nothing while Washington ignored the crisis was no longer acceptable. Testifying before the Senate Homeland Security Committee, Sheriff Dever summed up the mood of Arizonans well: "We cannot sit by while our citizens are terrorized, robbed, and murdered by ruthless and desperate people who enter our country illegally."

The Arizona ranchers—the cattlemen, as they are known— are the salt of the earth. They're the men and women who built Arizona and the American West. They're the rugged, independent-minded Americans Teddy Roosevelt looked to when he created his Rough Riders during the Spanish-American War. These are some of the toughest people you will ever know, and they had been living in fear. When I was secretary of state, I attended many meetings with the ranchers on the border. Illegal immigration was the number-one topic. Families told me that they were under siege. People were afraid to let their kids play outside. They were walking around their homes armed with guns.

They can be outspoken, but Arizona ranchers like Rob Krentz aren't complainers. They're not takers. All they want is for the border to be secured and for their families, their neighbors, and their land to be protected. That's all they ever asked for. That's all they continue to ask for today. And although there are few in southern Arizona who doubt that Rob was a victim of the drug violence coming across the border from Mexico, justice has still not been done. But what's most amazing is that these remarkable people don't blame the ordinary Mexicans and Mexican Americans they know. They blame the leaders whose job it was to protect Rob Krentz in the first place. Rob's family, with their usual class and humanity, said it best in a statement issued after his death:

> *We hold no malice toward the Mexican people for this senseless act but do hold the political forces in this country and Mexico accountable for what has happened. Their disregard of our repeated pleas and warnings of impending violence towards our community fell on deaf ears shrouded in political correctness. As a result, we have paid the ultimate price for their negligence in credibly securing our border.*

We all knew what "political forces" the Krentz family was pointing to. For years, real immigration reform in Washington had been held up by demands for the euphemistically named "comprehensive reform." But we also knew what that meant.

That meant a repeat of the 1986 immigration amnesty, signed by my hero Ronald Reagan. Back then, border security and tough reforms were supposed to accompany the amnesty of millions of illegal aliens that was granted in the law. But security and reform never came, and the amnesty encouraged millions more illegal aliens to come to America, secure in the belief that amnesty for them was just around the corner. I couldn't do anything about that in 1986, but in 2009, as governor of Arizona, I could choose not to be one of the "political forces" that endangered the lives of people like Rob Krentz. I was more determined than ever, after I saw the courage and dignity his family showed following his death, to finally do something. It was too late for Rob, and I was sick about that. But no more Arizona families would suffer like his, not if I could help it.

I got a firsthand glimpse of the "political correctness" the Krentz family referred to about ten days later. New Mexico governor Bill Richardson expressed an interest in touring the border after Rob died, so I took him on a tour of the area. As we flew across the beautiful but ravaged landscape, Governor Richardson seemed to join in my sorrow and indignation. All I could think was that these people—my fellow Arizonans—didn't have to live like this. *Rob Krentz did not have to die.* When we finished the tour, speaking to the large media gaggle that met us on the landing field in Douglas, I echoed one more time the call that the Arizona ranchers and lawmakers from both parties had made so many times before. We needed help. "It's incumbent upon the federal government to respond," I said. "We cannot do it alone."

While the cameras were on, Governor Richardson joined me in my call for help. I remember being grateful for his public words of support but wishing his actions as governor tracked more with the tough talk he was serving up. Under Governor Richardson, New Mexico in 2003 began a policy of not requiring proof of residency to get a New Mexico driver's license. New Mexico has issued an estimated 80,000 licenses to foreign nationals under Richardson's policy, but they have no way of knowing whether these licenses have gone to illegal aliens, because they don't ask applicants about their immigration status.

I've always believed that this is an incredibly dangerous, wrongheaded policy. New Mexico had no idea to whom it was giving its driver's licenses—and, with them, the ability to board planes or buy chemicals and fertilizer and any number of things that are useful to a terrorist. In Arizona, Richardson's policy was making it more difficult for us to enforce our laws against illegal immigration, to ensure the integrity of our elections, and to put the rights and needs of legal, law-abiding residents above those of lawbreakers. I was, frankly, unconvinced to hear Governor Richardson talk about getting on the border-security bandwagon following Rob's death since his policies had encouraged illegal immigration for years.

This is what the Krentz family meant by "deaf ears shrouded in political correctness"—politicians like Bill Richardson talking out of both sides of their mouth, pretending to protect their citizens while they actively encouraged illegal immigration through their policies. These so-called leaders don't hear the calls from the people for border security because they don't want to hear them. If they hear them, they will be expected to do something about them, and that's the last thing they want to do.

• • •

In June, the *New York Times Magazine* ran a cover story by an illegal alien named Jose Antonio Vargas. It recounted his life coming to the United States from the Philippines under a fake passport when he was twelve, being supplied a fake green card, and growing up to become a Pulitzer Prize–winning journalist. Vargas described being undocumented in the United States as "going about my day in fear." I always found it interesting that the *Times* never gave such prominent treatment to Rob Krentz. He, too, lived in fear, but of a different kind. His fear wasn't that his green card would be discovered as fake. His fear was for his family and his neighbors. His fear was of the violence and lawlessness that eventually took his life.

The mainstream media were interested in Rob's story for a while, but mainly as an example of how the right-wingers out in Arizona exploited the issue to pass their right-wing laws. They never covered the story in any depth—they never put the same human face on Rob Krentz that they did for Jose Antonio Vargas, because to do so would have exposed not only the violence on the border created by thuggish illegal aliens but also the humanity and tolerance of people like the Krentzes who believe the border should be secured. In the liberal media's view of the world, violent illegal aliens and tolerant supporters of the rule of law run counter to the story they want to tell, so they pretend they don't exist.

Instead, immigration is often portrayed as a tale of good versus evil, a political and cultural battle that pits two different visions of America against each other. One is the vision of America in which it's our moral obligation to absorb virtually unlimited numbers of poor, uneducated immigrants. Those who hold this view are the good guys—the ones who cherish and defend America's welcoming and generous spirit. The other vision, in the media's black-and-white interpretation, is the restrictionist view. In this vision, consciously or unconsciously racist Americans (there can be no other motive) seek an airtight border in order to preserve their western, white privilege. These, needless to say, are the bad guys. There's no middle ground in this popular media narrative; there are no "good guys" who believe we still need to control our border, and no "bad guys" who aren't racists and nativists.

Needless to say, this is a cartoon version of the problem we face on our border. It's also just one reason why so many Americans view the press as at best unreliable and at worst nakedly partisan. The overwhelming majority of Americans want to do the right thing, both for our country and for law-abiding newcomers. That means, for most of us, securing our border first and then—and only then—figuring out how to fix our broken immigration system. As I like to say, you don't call the architect when your house catches fire. You call the fire department. Later, you can get to the job of rebuilding.

Even those Americans for whom immigration seems a distant issue don't fall so easily into the open-borders-versus-closed-borders dynamic, no matter how hard the media and Washington try to shoehorn them in. As polls have shown, most Americans favor getting control of *illegal* immigration but continue to support being open to *legal* immigration. They understand the distinction between illegal and legal immigration—between honoring the law and not—that eludes much of the media. And for those of us who live and breathe illegal immigration every day, the issue is far from a simple tale of good guys versus bad guys. It's a practical, pressing issue of security and quality of life. For us, illegal immigration boils down to a few basic questions:

First, do our laws mean what they say they mean? Often lost

in the heat of the immigration debate is this undeniable fact: Crossing the border into the United States without the proper documentation is against the law. Period. We can either honor this law or we can abolish it. But our political leaders in Washington seem to uphold the law only when it suits them. The problem is, selectively honoring the law serves to undermine *all* of our laws. What's more, breaking the law to come to the United States too often leads to other law breaking. Employers break the law by hiring illegal aliens. And then the illegal aliens break the law by obtaining and using false identification—as do those who supply these documents. And that's just for starters. Illegal immigration is feeding a growing violent subculture of drug and human smuggling in the Southwest—a culture that is spreading across the country as they are beginning to diversify into other criminal activity like extortion and racketeering—just like the mafia. In the vacuum left by unenforced immigration laws, a new kind of organized crime is coming to America.

Second, who gets to decide who becomes an American? Should it be the criminals who profit from smuggling drugs and humans across our border? Should it be the immigrants who cut the line to come here illegally? Or should the citizens who make the laws and pay the taxes decide who their fellow citizens will be? Americans have different views on whether there should be more immigration or less to our country. I happen to believe that we should keep our borders open to legal immigrants. But few are neutral on the question of *who decides* who is admitted to our country. Illegal immigration takes this decision from the citizens and puts it in the hands of others; it takes it from the law-abiding and puts it in the hands of lawbreakers. No country in the history of the world has ever willingly done that and survived.

Finally, we come to the question that really hits home for me and my fellow Arizonans: Who will pay the costs of uncontrolled illegal immigration? The hundreds of thousands of mostly poor, mostly uneducated illegal aliens who enter this country every year impose real costs on our communities. The sick need health care. The hungry need to eat. The young need to be educated. While many Americans mistakenly believe that illegal aliens are ineligible for public services, many do receive benefits, mostly through their U.S.-born children. And then there is the cost of the crime and violence that increasingly accompanies illegal immigration.

Who's going to pay for all this? The communities and states that just happen to be along the border? Or the federal government whose job it is to protect the border and enforce the law? (That is, if we decide that our laws should be enforced to begin with!)

These are the real, unavoidable questions that Americans who live along the southwestern border have to deal with every day. The degree to which our leaders in Washington fail to consider these questions is beyond distressing. They seem to prefer to treat immigration as a purely political exercise. They look at it in terms of the votes they will gain or lose, not the individuals whose lives and property are destroyed. They look at it as a way to buy favor with this or that special interest group, not as a fundamental question of our national security and sovereignty. They look at it in terms of their self-interest in political advancement, not in terms of our national interest in the rule of law.

The failure of Washington to take illegal immigration seriously does a disservice to Arizonans and the people of the border states, of course. Unlike those who pontificate about the issue from Washington, New York, and other far-off centers of power and influence, we live with this problem every day. And like the Arizona ranchers who blame "political forces" on both sides of the border for fueling it and making it worse, we border-state Americans are angry about it.

But illegal immigration is not just "our problem" anymore—it is also yours. Increasingly, border states like Arizona are, for illegal aliens, simply transit points to cities and towns across the United States. The organized crime and drug and human smuggling rings that control the flow of humans across the border don't limit their North American operations to the Southwest. As we will see, they are global operations, bringing illegal crossers from all over the world into Mexico and then funneling them through Arizona to destinations in virtually every state in the union. And as go the criminals who run these organizations, so goes the violence, exploitation, and lawlessness that accompanies them. Americans in every state must wonder how a federal government that has grown so big and increasingly asserts its authority to interfere in every aspect of our lives can be so impotent in the face of a clear threat to our security and safety.

The irony is that the crisis of illegal immigration in Arizona is due in large part to our success at stopping it in other states along the southwestern border. That's right, folks: We *can* secure our border if we just summon the will to do so. We've done it before. We can do it again.

In the early 1990s, 75 percent of all illegal crossings along the 1,951-mile Mexican border occurred in San Diego or El Paso. Arizona was barely in the running. It was then that the U.S. government made the conscious decision to redirect illegal aliens east from San Diego and west from Texas by shoring up the border in these two locations. The idea was to push illegal crossers into more remote areas where they would have to make long, arduous crossings and would presumably be easier to apprehend. But it was an imperfect solution, and it came at a price for our state. As the *Los Angeles Times* acknowledged in 1993, "Arizona would bear the brunt of redirected migratory patterns, experts say."

In other words: California and Texas get more secure borders. Arizona doesn't. Washington decides; the rest of us just have to live with it.

It's already getting hard to remember what a problem it once was, but San Diego used to be a major transit point for illegal crossers. There was kind of a carnival atmosphere at the border. Vendors sold food, and impromptu soccer games broke out as thousands of would-be immigrants gathered near San Ysidro to make their break. They would wait until dark and then make a treacherous but brazen run across the eight-lane Interstate 5 freeway. It got so bad that the state of California put up signs showing the silhouette of a man, woman, and child to warn motorists to watch out for people crossing the highway.

By 1994 the people of San Diego were tired of illegal aliens darting in front of them in traffic and running through their backyards. Californians decided they had had enough. So their political leadership, aided by the Clinton administration, launched the project known as Operation Gatekeeper. A fourteen-mile fence with eight-foot-high steel panels was built in the San Diego area. Then another fence was constructed. Hundreds of new border agents were added to the area. Stadium lighting, infrared night scopes, and motion sensors were installed. The result was dramatic. Apprehensions of illegal aliens dropped from 524,231 in 1995 to 126,908 in 2005 in the sixty-six-mile San Diego sector. Federal and local officials also reported that rapes, killings, and other violent crimes sharply declined.

The effects of shoring up the border in El Paso were equally dramatic. Once again, when the political will is summoned to secure the border, it can be done. The El Paso sector, running from the Arizona–New Mexico state line all the way through the two westernmost counties in Texas, used to be a busy spot for illegal crossings. In the twenty miles of border between El Paso and Ciudad Juarez, an estimated 8,000 illegal aliens crossed each day. But about the same time California's border security was beefed up, the feds boosted security around El Paso. Operation Hold the Line gave up on the failed strategy of trying to catch illegal aliens after they'd entered the United States and instead focused on preventing them from entering in the first place. It reassigned agents to the border from other duties and doubled the number of Border Patrol agents. Apprehensions went from about 1,000 per day to 150 per day. Crime declined, as did human-rights-violation charges against the Border Patrol. The operation enjoyed broad support, including from the Mexican American community.

California and Texas are real-life refutations of the lie that securing our border is an impossible dream. The major downside of their success, however, is that it created a funnel effect, squeezing the flow of illegal aliens from the west and the east until it formed a gushing stream right through—you guessed it—Arizona. Now, California and Texas haven't solved their illegal immigration problems, not by a long stretch. But even their limited success has meant that hundreds of thousands of illegals who still want to cross the border every year now have to go through my state. Arizona has become the path of least resistance—the chokepoint through which illegal aliens enter the United States every year and then fan out across the country.

Of all the states in the union, Arizona is the site of the most illegal crossings. More illegal aliens are detained in Arizona—and more drugs are confiscated in Arizona—than in any other state. Although the numbers have declined overall since the onset of the recession, the federal government currently estimates that about half of all illegal border crossings—of *all* borders in America—are through the Grand Canyon State. This is a considerable change from 1992, when fewer than 8 percent were recorded in Arizona. In 2009, Customs and Border Protection apprehended almost as many illegal aliens in Arizona as in California and Texas *combined*. That year, the Border Patrol caught more than 550,000 illegal aliens, and over 240,000 of these apprehensions occurred in the Tucson sector. Since 2009, well over 400,000 people have crossed illegally into the United States in the Tucson sector—the equivalent, according to Arizona Attorney General Tom Horne, of an invasion of twenty divisions.

As if that weren't bad enough, the Border Patrol estimates that it apprehends only one in four illegal border crossers. That means the actual number crossing into Arizona every year is at least a million. That's about twice the population of the city of Tucson. And for every illegal immigrant who's a criminal and who gets arrested crossing the border—a gang member, a drug dealer, even a child molester—three are missed and find their way into neighborhoods in other states all across America.

So it's not for nothing that parts of Arizona have been called lawless free-for-alls when it comes to illegal immigration. And the reason is not that law enforcement and Border Patrol agents are failing to do their job. These men and women are being threatened, shot at, sometimes paying the ultimate price, and still doing a heroic service for their communities and their country.

No, the reason for the crisis of illegal immigration is that our *leaders in Washington* are failing to do their job. Despite their protests that the border is "as secure as it's ever been," the experts tell a different story.

The federal government's own independent research group, the Government Accountability Office (GAO), admits that of the nearly 2,000 miles of border between the United States and Mexico, less than 44 percent is under the "operational control" of the Border Patrol. As if that isn't bad enough, consider that the feds define "operational control" as not necessarily the ability to locate and apprehend illegal aliens at the border itself, but *up to 100 miles from the border.* In fact, only 15 percent of the border is under full control in the sense that crossers are caught then and there.

Fifteen percent. If 15 percent in control means the border is "as secure as it's ever been," we're in bigger trouble than even I realized.

Arizona has dealt with the challenge of illegal immigration for a long time. Mexico is our neighbor, after all. And like all neighbors, we have had good times and bad. But for the most part, for those of us who have lived, worked, and raised families in the Southwest, our Mexican neighbors are people like us. Most of them want what we want: to provide for their families and live in safety and security.

But a few years ago, Arizonans began to notice a change in the character of many of the people crossing the border. Although most illegal aliens were still just looking for an opportunity to provide for their families, another, more sinister type was now haunting the border. As usual, it was the people who live along the border itself, like Rob Krentz, who noticed it first.

The cattlemen told us that more and more of the illegal aliens they saw on their land were no longer wearing their traditional clothes. Now they were wearing black—they even painted their water jugs black—to be less detectable at night. And instead of carrying Circle K plastic bags with their shoes and other personal items like they used to, more and more were carrying automatic weapons. Homes were being broken into. Women at home alone during the day reported menacing men staring at their houses and refusing to leave. Rob Krentz himself made the observation to a group of ranchers around that time that if something didn't change, it was inevitable that someone would be killed.

Up in the interior of the state, we realized that things had changed for the worse when violence spiked in places like Phoenix. In 2003 alone, we had a 45 percent rise in homicides that the police traced to fighting among gangs smuggling drugs and illegal aliens and a 400 percent rise in kidnappings, home invasions, and extortion linked to illegals.

A home invasion is every bit as terrifying as the name suggests. Rival drug gang members have been known to dress in uniforms similar to those of the Phoenix police and carry military-style rifles to target homes of other smugglers where they believe large amounts of cash, drugs, or weapons are stored.

During the attacks, residential neighborhoods have been sprayed with hundreds of rounds of automatic-weapon fire. Earlier this year, eight armed men broke into a west Phoenix home at three A.M. looking for drugs while a mother and father and their six-year-old daughter were asleep. They beat and stabbed the father, and one of the intruders died in a shoot-out with police. Since then, stories of home invasions and the ensuing armed clashes with police have become routine in the Phoenix area.

And of course, we started to find more bodies along the roadside and in the desert, the innocent and not-so-innocent victims of the growing violence entering our state from the southern border.

I vividly remember the crisp November morning in 2003 when we got one of the first of many wake-up calls about this new and very frightening level of violence. I was at my office in the Capitol when reports started coming in that Department of Public Safety officers had come upon bodies scattered along the median of Interstate 10 southeast of Phoenix. They were the grisly remains of a forty-mile, high-speed shoot-out between illegal-alien-smuggling gangs.

I did a mental inventory of everyone I knew who might have been traveling along I-10 that morning. As the details came in, each was more unbelievable then the next. The shootings had occurred at eight thirty in the morning. In broad daylight. During rush-hour traffic on a well-traveled interstate highway. Four people were believed to be dead.

What happened was this: After crossing the border with a group of illegals, a human-smuggling gang had its "cargo" hijacked by a rival gang about eighty-five miles from the border, just north of Tucson. The two groups of smugglers, with the robbers and their human cargo in the lead, took off heading northwest on I-10 toward Phoenix. The original smugglers caught up with the rip-off gang just north of Casa Grande, about thirty miles from Phoenix. They pulled up alongside them and opened fire—still speeding up the freeway—with automatic weapons. The back-and-forth gunfight continued along the freeway for more than thirty miles, until they ran into the morning rush-hour traffic heading into Phoenix. The vehicles were so shot up that police found one man crouched by the side of the highway, holding the toe that had been blown off his foot in the gunfire.

Looking back, it's clear that the I-10 freeway shooting was just a taste of things to come. Smuggling humans across the border had become big business. So much money was at stake—and so little risk of capture or lengthy incarceration was involved—that rival groups had taken to stealing each other's "cargo." But not only were the lives of illegal aliens being lost, but the lives of Arizonans themselves were being threatened. Even now, I look back and shudder at the thought of someone I love being caught in the crossfire that morning.

The rapid growth of human smuggling in the Southwest desert is first of all a tale of human greed. At critical points, the criminals that operate along the border saw potential for yet more money to be made off of human misery, and at each point the levels of violence and suffering increased. Along the way, it became a story about something else as well: a story of total indifference to the sanctity of life.

But perhaps the worst part of the story is our government's utter failure to protect us from this evil. A government's most fundamental job is to protect its citizens from those who prey upon the vulnerable and put profit above human life. The outrage of human smuggling in America isn't just that these kinds of criminals exist. It's that our federal government has chosen to ignore them for so long.

Once upon a time, Mexicans, Central Americans, or others seeking to cross the border into the United States illegally might pay a "mom-and-pop" guide a few hundred dollars to help them across. But the security crackdowns following the attacks of September 11, 2001, made crossing America's borders, for a time, more dangerous and difficult. Where illegal aliens used to slip across relatively easily with the help of small-time guides—commonly known by their Spanish name, *coyotes*—after 9/11 the crossing got more perilous. Illegal aliens could still cross, but now they needed more help. Greater danger meant greater demand for *coyotes*, and that, of course, meant higher prices. These higher prices in turn attracted a more organized, sophisticated, and brutal criminal element.

By that memorable morning of the I-10 shoot-out, mom-and-pop smuggling operations had largely been replaced by cold-blooded, high-stakes, organized criminal gangs. And instead of moving individuals or small groups of illegals, these gangs are responsible for smuggling thousands of illegal aliens into Arizona each day.

Human smuggling is a multibillion-dollar business in Arizona and the Southwest. Today, organized smuggling operations can command anywhere from $2,000 to $3,000 per person—and much more if the illegal immigrant is from China, Central Europe, or any country other than Mexico. They deal in bulk, herding groups of twenty, fifty, or a hundred people at a time.

As it stands, the risk these smugglers take is nothing compared with the money they can make. They can average $2,000 a head smuggling a hundred people across the border up to three times a week. You do the math.

As if this weren't bad enough, something else has happened to the cross-border traffic in human beings that has made it even more dangerous: The Mexican drug cartels have gotten involved. In retrospect, it's easy to see that it was only a matter of time before this happened. If you can move humans across the border, you can also move drugs; it doesn't take a genius to see the enormous profits that can be made by combining the two. So, increasingly, the drug cartels are turning aliens seeking to cross the border—even those who just want to come to the United States to work—into reluctant drug mules. Double the illegality—quadruple the money. The GAO has estimated that the Mexican cartels earned $8 billion to $23 billion from U.S. drug sales in 2005 alone. At the high end, reported the *Arizona Republic*, that puts the Mexican cartels at ninety-seventh on the Fortune 500 list, just below Coca-Cola.

Law enforcement officials tasked with detecting and dismantling these operations tell us that the cartels will typically take a group of illegal crossers, isolate the healthy males, and "make them pack," as they say. For the most part, these immigrants are poor, desperate people. They are in no position to resist the demands of armed, bloodthirsty gangsters who offer them the infamous choice of *plata o plomo*—silver or lead. So each crosser is forced to carry, say, a backpack containing fifty to sixty pounds of marijuana. The cartels use duct tape to secure the backpack so completely that the immigrant can't remove it—they're literally taped into their drug loads. Then they are marched sixty or seventy miles across the border and through the desert up to one of the major interstate highways that parallel the border in Arizona, I-8 or I-10.

These crossings can take days, and they are very dangerous. In remote areas of Arizona, like the Tohono O'odham Indian reservation, you can walk through the desert for hours without seeing any people, roads, or buildings. There are rattlesnakes and scorpions. The sun is relentless, and water is nonexistent. Here, an injury—even a slight one—can mean the difference between life and death. Drug-cartel *coyotes* think nothing of leaving behind the sick or injured, and the Border Patrol routinely comes upon their decomposed remains.

When they reach the interstate, the smuggling bands are usually met by gang members with vehicles. Before they are piled into the trucks, vans, or SUVs, the illegal immigrants' backpacks are literally cut off them. But the Mexican cartels are careful. They know better than to have their human and drug cargoes in the same place. So the drugs go off in one vehicle and the people in another.

It's along the interstates and back roads of Arizona that our law enforcement officers most often encounter illegal aliens. The smugglers' vehicles are typically in bad shape, and heavily laden, often with more than twenty people inside. They travel at high speeds, and rollovers are common. I remember when, a couple of years ago, an SUV carrying at least twenty-seven people rolled over around midnight on a remote stretch of highway in southeastern Arizona. The reports said that the illegal aliens were "stacked like wood" in the back of the truck. Eight people, including the driver, were killed. Five had to be airlifted to a Tucson hospital.

The initial destination of human smugglers traveling along Arizona's roads and interstates, more often than not, is the Phoenix metropolitan area. But even when they reach Arizona's largest city, a couple hundred miles from the border, the mayhem isn't over. In many ways, it's just beginning.

Earlier this year, federal authorities raided a house in a quiet west Phoenix neighborhood of single-family homes. Inside the four-bedroom, two-and-a-half-bath house they found 108 frightened, dehydrated illegal aliens.

Welcome to Arizona's notorious drop houses.

A drop house is a house—very often rented—where smugglers hold their frightened charges until they have received enough payment from the immigrants or their families to let them go. Rarely does a week go by in Arizona that our newspapers and televisions don't carry news of law enforcement finding another drop house. In an unfortunate confluence of bad trends, the foreclosure crisis has combined with the immigration crisis to give smugglers their pick of homes in Phoenix and its surrounding suburbs. In Phoenix alone, law enforcement has discovered more than 600 drop houses in recent years. Many, many more go undetected. Meaning that, at any given time, literally thousands of people are being held hostage in these houses.

Coyotes used to hold illegal aliens in drop houses until they had paid the prearranged price of their crossing. The immigrants would use the place to rest, lie low, and pay their bills, and then were sent on to their final destination. But the more vicious breed of criminals who now control the human smuggling business sensed an opportunity. Why should they be satisfied with a

$2,000-to-$3,000 negotiated price when there's more money to be had, provided you don't have a conscience? So these criminals started to hold the migrants hostage, demanding additional cash payments from their relatives before they'd be released.

Today's drop houses have been described as prisons and torture houses. Captain Fred Zumbo, who heads the Department of Public Safety's illegal immigration task force, describes the men who run Phoenix's drop houses as "a violent subculture of twenty-to-thirty-year-old Mexican men who have no regard for human life and dignity." In addition to torturing the immigrants they smuggle, this subculture of criminals, Captain Zumbo told me, "puts citizens at risk."

Drop houses can be found anywhere, even in middle-class and upscale neighborhoods. Because they're so hard to detect, police often rely on tips from terrified relatives to find them. Sometimes they find drop houses by watching for a few telltale signs. Police watch the interstates for bulky, heavily laden vehicles that might be carrying large numbers of illegals. Very often, these vans and SUVs have temporary license plates, or tags from a stolen car. If the police get suspicious, they follow. Smugglers like to make their drops late at night, while the neighbors are asleep. If police see the weighted-down vehicle pull into the garage of a house, watch the garage door close, then see it open again a few minutes later as a suddenly lighter vehicle emerges, they know they're on to something.

What goes on inside these houses is literally the stuff of a horror movie. Immigrants are beaten, they are raped, they are Tasered, and they are murdered. Smugglers pack them in, forty, fifty, sixty, and more to a house. Dozens of human beings are shoehorned into rooms in which the furniture has been removed and the windows boarded up. To prevent their escape, the immigrants are sometimes forced to remove their clothes. On one memorable night in 2008, Captain Zumbo's task force responded to a Phoenix police report of fifty naked, bloody people running down the street. They were a group of illegal aliens that had overpowered their guard and busted out of a drop house by breaking through the back patio doors.

Captain Zumbo told me about one undocumented Mexican man who was running a very violent—but tragically typical—drop house. Like other smugglers, this guy was as clever as he was sadistic. The smugglers know that most people seeking to enter the United States have relatives here. And those relatives have money. So this guy would take those immigrants who he suspected had lucrative connections in the United States to a boarded-up "torture room" within the drop house. He would call their relatives on the phone and demand $3,000 in exchange for the immigrants' lives. Then he would take a wooden dowel—a cylindrical piece of wood not unlike a baseball bat—and beat the men. The relatives would listen on the phone as the men were beaten and begged for their lives. What would anyone do in that situation? The relatives would pay to free their loved ones, and the torturer would get rich. And that's what happens in anonymous drop houses in Phoenix and across the country every day. People suffer and criminals get rich. The ones that we've discovered are just the tip of the iceberg. The smugglers tell illegal aliens that their families in the United States and Mexico will be targeted if they tell the police. And for good reason, the immigrants believe them.

The evidence that Phoenix has become the drop-house-and-kidnapping capital of America can be found outside the police reports as well. After 9/11, wire transfer businesses were required to report data on senders and receivers to state attorneys general, so we took a look at what was reported for Arizona. The result was astounding. The data showed that Arizona is a magnet for money transfers, with a great deal of money coming in and very little going out. Delaware, for example, sent sixty times as much to Arizona as Arizona sent to Delaware. South Carolina wired thirty-eight times as much cash to Arizona as Arizonans sent there. In all, the wire transfers entering the state dwarf the transfers leaving it by a factor of thirty. What that tells us is obvious: A lot of people are paying a lot of money to bring illegal aliens safely into our country.

The most recent phase of the escalating violence has been its most violent yet. This is the stage in which the stakes become so high that the criminals turn on each other. It is the point at which the amounts of money being made are so great that, criminals being criminals, they start to prey on one another. Smugglers start to rob smugglers. Drug dealers steal from drug dealers. And freelance criminal gangs organize to rip off both. This is where Arizona is today, and where much of America may be tomorrow.

The driving force behind the criminal-on-criminal violence is simple: Human beings and drugs are both more valuable to criminals on the U.S. side of the border than they are on the Mexican side. After all, our side is where drugs can be sold, and where illegal aliens want to be. In the eyes of the criminal class, the value of both drugs and people is very little before they cross the border. But once across, their value soars, and the loads of illegal aliens, drugs, and the cash they bring become ripe targets for thieves.

The Spanish slang that surrounds the human-smuggling trade probably best describes the rise of intra-criminal violence on the border. If illegal aliens are *pollos*, or chickens, and human smugglers are *polleros*, or chicken ranchers, the thieves who rip off the smugglers are known as *bajadores*—chicken thieves.

Bajadores are typically illegal aliens themselves. They're opportunistic rather than organized, but they are heavily armed. Their motive is money, pure and simple. Like the thieves in the I-10 shootout, they kidnap loads of illegal immigrants from smugglers and hold them for ransom. According to police, immigrants typically fetch $1,500 to $2,500 a head. Not infrequently, these criminals kidnap their competition. Kidnapped smugglers pay off at $10,000 to $50,000 each. Thanks to criminals preying largely on criminals, Phoenix now has the dubious distinction of being the kidnapping capital of America, second in the world only to Mexico City. And recent audits indicate that Phoenix officials have actually underreported the number of kidnappings in Phoenix.

Sometimes these gangs simply zero in on a drop house, break in, kill the guards, and start taking over the payments made by the illegal immigrants. Other times they will discover a house where they think people, drugs, or cash are being held, arm themselves with military-style rifles, dress up like police officers or SWAT teams, and raid the house.

For these guys, anything they get is pure profit.

But more dangerous than even the loosely organized *bajadores* are the rival Mexican drug cartels whose brutal fights to control smuggling routes and market share are increasingly spilling over from Mexico into the United States.

By now most Americans are familiar with the out-of-control violence in Mexico related to the drug wars. The murder and mayhem there are truly beyond comprehension. But even this incomprehensible violence has a purpose. Forty thousand Mexican citizens have been killed since President Felipe Calderón began his campaign against the cartels in December 2006; but for the drug cartels, this has not been enough. They have moved beyond murder in their viciousness and brutality. Cartels routinely mutilate victims for no obvious reason. And they don't "just" behead their victims anymore. They skin them and rip their hearts from their chests. In one case, the cartels actually cut the face off a victim and stitched it to a soccer ball. Law enforcement officials agree that this is done to send a message both to the Mexican people and to the other cartels. To the first: The government is powerless to help you. And to the second: Don't cross us.

The lifeblood of these cartels, of course, is the smuggling routes across the U.S. border. These are literally their livelihoods, their superhighways to outrageous fortune. As a consequence, the cartels seek to control these routes using any means necessary. The mountaintops of the Southwest desert are infested with hundreds of so-called spotters—cartel members who monitor the smuggling routes for other cartels, *bajadores*, and the Border Patrol. Two to three hundred of these spotters are in the hills—deep inside U.S. territory—at any given time. They use radios to communicate with smugglers leading human trains of drug mules across the desert, letting them know if it is safe to pass or if thieves or rivals are on their route.

Despite the fact that they squat in primitive caves called "spider holes" for months at a time, the spotters are highly sophisticated. They have the usual high-powered weapons, including, in at least one case, shoulder-fired rocket launchers. They use (and leave behind) car batteries to power their encrypted satellite radios. Sometimes they even use solar panels. They have GPS and night-vision goggles to monitor the smuggling routes. If they see a U.S. official or a rival gang member, sometimes they just report it. Sometimes they shoot.

And, sad as it is to say, the cartels have established a degree of control over the border that the United States government has never come close to having. I remember reading a story in the *Dallas Morning News* about a drug cartel that was waging war on another smuggling ring for control of a route in the Tucson sector. The reporter had talked to one man who wanted to come to the States for a construction job but couldn't. The border, the man told the newspaper, was *"tapado por la mafia"*—closed by the mafia. "There's too much vigilance, too much," he said. "And it's not the border patrol."

The "vigilance" of the drug cartels is making the Mexican mafia very rich, and the American Southwest increasingly dangerous. The cartels now control the U.S. markets for marijuana, cocaine, and methamphetamine, and they are moving more and more of it across the border. The amount of marijuana seized by the Border Patrol in 2010 was more than 3 million pounds, with an estimated street value of over $2 billion. That's *billion* with a *b*. During the past two years, the amount of marijuana seized by Sheriff Paul Babeu's office in Pinal County—which is seventy miles from the border—more than doubled. The trend that is truly alarming is how the smuggling of hard-core drugs has skyrocketed—cocaine is up 90 percent, heroin is up 40 percent, and methamphetamine is up 20 percent.

And despite the Obama administration's claims to the contrary, the cartels are bringing violence across the border along with their drugs. Border Patrol agent Brian Terry was killed earlier this year in a gunfight linked to the cartels. The cartels are now openly threatening law enforcement. Jeffrey Kirkham, chief of police in the border town of Nogales, reports that his officers have been threatened. Informants in the cartels have told Chief Kirkham to ignore cross-border drug shipments or pay the price.

Along with drugs and violence, the cartels are bringing their unique criminal methods across the border as well. Just last year, their passion for beheadings became evident in the Phoenix area. Police entered an apartment in Chandler and found a head in one room and the body in another. And increasingly, the cartels are recruiting American citizens to join in their criminal activity. Earlier this year, on the Tohono O'odham reservation, federal agents and tribal police arrested forty-six people accused of working with the Mexican cartels that use their land to smuggle people and drugs. The cartels are even recruiting Arizona high school kids—American citizens—to do their dirty work. They pay them $200 or so to use their parents' cars to transport drugs across the border. Eventually these kids typically drop out of school because the money is so good. They effectively become members of the cartel. And if they want out, the cartels won't let them go—once they're in, they're in for life, however long that lasts.

In addition to the drug cartels, Arizona is plagued by garden-variety criminals sneaking in from Mexico. Each week, U.S. Customs and Border Protection publishes a report of the arrests made in the area near Tucson. Recent reports detail arrests of illegal aliens who are gang members. Some have previous criminal convictions for crimes against children, including child molestation. It's easy for federal officials with political motives to sit in Washington, D.C., and tell us we're exaggerating the criminal threat coming across the border and insinuate that we're racists and xenophobes. But we see it every day. We live it every day. And we have had enough.

All of this violence and illegality has a cost, of course. The most important and immediate cost of our unsecured border is paid by people, both Americans and immigrants, in their lives, their health, and their safety.

For many of the immigrants attempting to cross our border, the cost is very high indeed. Last July, illegal alien deaths were so high that the Pima County Medical Examiner's Office had to use a refrigerated truck to store some of the bodies. In the first seven months of 2010, the Pima County authorities recovered 140 bodies—59 in July alone. Since 2001, the bodies of more than 2,100 men, women, and children have been found in the Arizona desert. Even as federal authorities report that border apprehensions are down, border deaths keep climbing. For me, that's not an indication that our border is "as secure as it's ever been." Growing border deaths are an indication of precisely the opposite. Regardless of your position on immigration, these deaths on sovereign U.S. soil should sadden and shame us all.

For those of us who live near the border, the cost is the very real threat to the safety of our families and communities. Some pay more than others. Rob Krentz and Border Patrol agent Brian Terry are two tragic examples. But all of us feel the pain and insecurity that comes with seeing our wonderful, diverse state, with its warm, welcoming people and its unique natural beauty, overtaken by lawlessness. All of us lose a measure of our freedom because of this federal failure.

Illegal immigration costs us in more tangible ways as well. One of the frequently overlooked burdens of illegal immigration is the tremendous environmental damage done by the hundreds of thousands of people who traipse across the border each year.

The piles of trash left behind in the desert by illegal immigration have to be seen to be believed. Each illegal alien who crosses is said to leave about six to eight pounds of trash along the way. That adds up to more than 2,000 tons of trash each year. In 2006 alone, over a million pounds of trash was picked up along the Arizona border. Some of it is heart-breaking stuff: wedding pictures, photos of children, baby blankets. But most of it is just an eyesore. Illegal aliens and their smugglers leave behind veritable mountains of water bottles, backpacks, food wrappers, used diapers, and human excrement. Even cars and trucks are abandoned by smugglers and left on the border. The trash is everywhere, but it's typically concentrated in what are called "lay-up" spots—places where illegal aliens rest and wait for the next smuggler to guide them farther north. Federal and state agencies, ranchers, and volunteers conduct massive cleanups, but the trash just keeps on coming.

The irony is that much of the land along the U.S. side of the Arizona border is supposedly protected by the federal government for environmental and historic reasons. Federal laws like the Endangered Species Act and the National Environmental Policy Act restrict access to the land. To enter these protected lands, the Border Patrol has to wait and get special permission from federal bureaucrats. Sometimes four months pass before permission is granted! That means the Border Patrol can't police these areas effectively, so more illegal aliens get through, leaving more trash. In the twisted world of illegal immigration, environmentally protected lands suffer more damage than unprotected ones. It got so bad that Rob Krentz's widow, Sue, asked the government not to classify wilderness areas as protected in order to protect them from illegal immigration.

Millions of dollars have been spent in Arizona cleaning up the trash left by illegal immigration. But that amount is nothing compared with the burden on Arizona taxpayers created by illegal aliens once they settle in our state. Our education, health care, and incarceration systems are strained past the limit. We've done what we could through ballot measures and a 2009 law I signed requiring proof of eligibility for state services. But many of the most costly parts of the American welfare state are mandated by the federal government. Moreover, simple Christian compassion requires that human beings in need get medical care, that children be housed, fed, and educated. Arizonans have generously met this humane obligation, but Arizona can't continue to sustain it, because of our uncontrolled borders. And increasingly, as illegal aliens pass through Arizona and fan out across the country, our burden is becoming America's burden.

The cost of incarcerating the criminals who cross our border is by itself astronomical. Law enforcement officials across the state have done a magnificent job in a very trying circumstance. But in the process they've caught a lot of bad guys, and these bad guys have to go somewhere. The result is that the Arizona Department of Corrections incarcerates some 6,000 criminal aliens, nearly 17 percent of our inmate population. Of the felony defendants in Maricopa County, 21.8 percent are illegal aliens. The cost to the Arizona taxpayers is approximately $150 million every year. The federal government is responsible for picking up much of this tab, but it has utterly refused to do so. I have—unsuccessfully so far—constantly begged the Obama administration to deliver to Arizona taxpayers the more than $880 million it owes us. And I haven't been alone. My colleague in Texas, Rick Perry, recently sent the federal government a bill for $349 million for the state and local cost of incarcerating illegal aliens in Texas. In a letter to Homeland Security Secretary Janet Napolitano, Governor Perry noted that the State Criminal Alien Assistance Program (SCAAP), created to reimburse states for the cost of locking up criminal aliens, "doesn't begin to compensate the entirety of Texas's financial burden." When Napolitano was governor, she would annually hold press conferences demanding payment with a giant cardboard prop—an oversize invoice for President George W. Bush. Now she's busy defending the current administration's refusal to honor its commitments. As usual, Arizona taxpayers are left footing the bill.

Add to the cost of incarcerating criminal aliens the court costs involved in prosecuting cases. According to recent reports, illegal reentry—attempting to reenter the United States illegally after already having been caught at least once—was the most frequent federal crime charged in the first six months of 2010, and the same held true for Arizona. The good news is that the number of these charges being brought in Arizona is increasing; the bad news is that it costs money. According to the University of Arizona study, from 1999 through 2006, the twenty-four counties along the U.S.-Mexico border spent a total of $1.23 billion on processing illegal aliens through the criminal justice system. The Arizona border counties spend over $26 million of taxpayer money every year providing law enforcement and criminal justice services, such as public defenders for illegal aliens.

Not all of the people crossing illegally into Arizona come here for the purpose of committing additional crimes, of course. They are admirable, hardworking souls who want nothing more than a better life for their families. But they are also overwhelmingly poor and uneducated. Studies show that welfare use is correlated with education level. Both native-born and immigrant Americans with college degrees earn about the same amount. And immigrants with college degrees contribute more in taxes than they consume in public services.

The problem is, in Arizona, around half of the illegal aliens entering the state have less than a high school education. The result is that nearly a third of all Arizonans living in poverty are in immigrant households. And of these households, two thirds are headed by at least one illegal alien. Their use of public assistance has nothing to do with their willingness to work—and work hard. Most immigrant households have at least one member who is working. But too often, it's not enough.

These generally hardworking, law-abiding immigrants nonetheless place a crushing burden on Arizona taxpayers. The costs to Arizona taxpayers of illegal immigration fall into three broad categories: health care, education, and law enforcement.

Federal law requires that hospitals provide treatment in emergency rooms to anyone, regardless of immigration status or ability to pay the bill. Many people, particularly the uninsured, use hospitals for non-emergencies. And because approximately 60 percent of illegal immigrants are uninsured, as illegal immigration has soared in Arizona, so has the cost of providing emergency room care. Between 2001 and 2005, emergency room visits for outpatient care spiked by 46 percent in Arizona while they increased by only 8 percent nationally. Emergency room personnel don't ask about the legal status of their patients, so nailing down the numbers is hard. But a 2002 report mandated by Arizona senator Jon Kyl found that hospitals and ambulances in the border counties of Arizona, California, New Mexico, and Texas spent more than $200 million in one year on emergency medical treatment of illegal aliens. In Arizona, the cost was $31 million. Thanks to Internet sites that tell illegal aliens how to claim care at American hospitals—complete with maps showing where to find them—the cost of uncompensated care in Arizona hospitals for non-citizen immigrants in 2004 was more than $135 million. Our total Medicaid costs to this group were over $475 million. The federal government—meaning, the American taxpayers—covers much of these costs. But in total, in fiscal year 2011, the costs of providing illegal aliens with federally mandated emergency medical care, Medicaid, cash assistance, youth and family services, and other health and welfare benefits were almost $200 million.

Educating illegal aliens and their U.S.-born children is another area of high cost to Arizona taxpayers. According to the Pew Center, as many as 170,000 Arizona students, out of a total student population just over 1 million, have parents who are illegal aliens. And it's not only the cost of educating illegal aliens we've had to pay in our schools: until former Arizona schools chief Tom Horne put a stop to it in 2010, for years Mexican children were actually being picked up every day and bused across the border to attend Arizona public schools in Ajo, forty miles north of the border!

Most of these children are struggling to learn English, which adds to the cost. In 2009 the Supreme Court ruled in favor of Arizona in a long and costly legal battle over funding English Language Learners (ELL) in our public schools.

Still, the cost of our approximately 170,000 ELL students in 2008 was about a $70 million drain on the taxpayers, and the ELL cost in 2009 was more than $110 million. In total, the cost to the state of educating undocumented children was $1.2 billion in FY 2011.

Adding the cost of imprisoning criminal aliens brings the total expense to Arizona taxpayers of illegal immigration in FY 2011 to about $1.6 billion. Even if we deduct the estimated $670 million illegal aliens will have paid in taxes this fiscal year, we still have a net cost to the Arizona taxpayers of almost $1 billion. Out of an $8.5 billion state budget—and in the middle of the biggest recession since the Great Depression—that's not chump change.

And as for those Americans living far away from the border who think they're immune to these problems: Think again. According to the Justice Department, the cartels have spread their violent reach to at least 230 American cities. They are, in the words of the U.S. government, "the greatest organized crime threat to the United States." The same cartels that kidnap, rape, and murder in Phoenix maintain drop houses in Georgia; conduct assaults in Alabama; engage in shootouts in the Pacific Northwest; and distribute marijuana, cocaine, methamphetamine, and heroin from Anchorage to Miami.

And just as the criminal element imposes costs on these communities, so does the level of illegal immigration itself. According to the Pew Hispanic Center, illegal aliens are more widely dispersed across the country than ever before. There were more than half a million illegal aliens in Illinois in 2010. There were

625,000 in the state of New York, 550,000 in New Jersey, 325,000 in North Carolina, and 425,000 in Georgia.

These populations impose tremendous costs on local taxpayers. According to the Center for Immigration Studies, welfare use by illegal aliens is highest in California, at 77 percent. But the state with the second-highest rate of welfare expenditures for illegal aliens is New York, far from the Mexican border, at 76 percent. The border state of Texas is next, with 70 percent of its illegal immigration population on welfare, but Illinois is close behind, at 68 percent. Minnesota, Georgia, and Nevada follow in highest welfare use by the undocumented, at 65 percent. Thanks to the high numbers of illegal aliens in our state and the federal mandates, Arizona comes next. If we hadn't limited state services, we would be much higher on the list.

For the taxpayers of these states and a growing number of others, the question of how to deal with the burden imposed by illegal immigration is not the media myth of good guys versus bad guys. It's no wonder, then, that so many of these states are considering or have already passed laws that mirror Arizona's tough immigration laws. Like us, they are facing a huge challenge. Like us, they've received from Washington the public-policy equivalent of the back of the hand. And like us, they are finally being forced to take matters into their own hands.

For many Americans, Rob Krentz's tragic death was their first real glimpse of the immigration crisis on our border. But it is a crisis that has been long in the making.

Despite what you may have heard, it's not a crisis of race or culture. It's a crisis of violence, desperation, and human greed.

It's a humanitarian crisis. An environmental crisis. An economic crisis. A political crisis. It's a crisis that the people who live and work along America's southwestern border know all too well. We didn't cause it. We didn't ask for it. But we've lived with it for years. And soon, unless our government acts, the entire country will be living with it, too.

Fueled by drugs and lawlessness, and abetted by federal indifference—or worse—Arizona's crisis is coming to the rest of America. In fact, it's already here.

CHAPTER TWO

Janbo

Arizona's image in the mainstream media has taken a pounding since I signed SB 1070. Opponents of the law have been determined to explain away its majority support (in Arizona and the rest of the country) as the product of racism. It's a cheap, easy, unsubstantiated accusation that is designed not to further debate but to shut it down. Instead of debating the merits of the law—or even reading it, in the case of Attorney General Eric Holder—the media and many Washington politicians prefer hysterical name calling.

For me, one of the many low points in this sordid national drama came when ABC took its hidden-camera show *What Would You Do?* to Tucson earlier this year. The show, in case you've never seen it, is a quasi news program that seems determined to cast the American people in the worst possible light. They use actors to stage scenes designed to bring out the meanness in people—a phony waitress refusing to serve actors playing gay patrons at a restaurant, or a dwarf at a convenience store being ridiculed by other actors playing insensitive shoppers. All the hateful, bigoted stuff is done by actors, mind you. The responses from real Americans are taped by hidden cameras.

As you can see, I'm not crazy about *What Would You Do?* It values the sensational and the confrontational over the truth and creates fake "news" designed to attract ratings. But the show's producers really outdid themselves when they came to Tucson. Under the pretext of examining the implications of SB 1070, they staged a phony scene in a restaurant with the wonderfully Arizonan name of BK Carne Asada & Hot Dogs. In the setup, actors playing Hispanic patrons were harassed by an actor playing a racist security guard. The guard demanded to see the customers' IDs as they stood in line for tacos and the restaurant's famous Sonoran-style hot dogs, saying he just wanted to make sure they were "legal." It was a grotesque distortion of the actual provisions of Arizona's immigration law—a lie of such magnitude that the Arizona Speaker of the House, Kirk Adams, later demanded that ABC apologize for airing the show. I, too, was outraged. SB 1070 gives no one the right to ask people standing in a restaurant for their identification, much less an off-duty security guard.

What the producers didn't count on was the reaction by the real-life Arizonans in the restaurant. Time and again, as the cameras rolled, unsuspecting Arizonans came to the aid of the people they thought were innocent, harassed Hispanics. They were outraged by the (fake) bigotry they witnessed. At one point it looked as if they were about to come to blows with the security guard, and a reporter was forced to step out of the shadows and admit it was all a setup. Everyone in the restaurant was good-natured about it when they found out the truth. I'll just say this: They took the deception better than I would have.

That obnoxious show stays with me, both for how grossly it distorted the law we passed and, more important, for the tolerance and caring it showed by Arizonans themselves. Liberal activists and their media accomplices can call Arizonans racist all they want, but when they brought in hidden cameras to record how we actually treat one another, Arizonans showed them otherwise.

This is the Arizona I know—the Arizona I've always known. After all, most Arizonans are (like me) from somewhere else. We've always been a state that welcomes outsiders. All we've asked is that people obey the law, respect their neighbors, and respect our state.

Now, it's true that the Arizona I know has an independent streak. We've always proudly and defiantly gone our own way. We haven't always danced to the tune set in Washington, New York, or Hollywood. No, we don't observe daylight saving time. And, yes, we honor the Second Amendment and allow law-abiding citizens to carry guns. But most of all, we respect and take care of one another as neighbors and fellow citizens. And that goes as much for the Hispanics whose families have been here since before statehood as the Anglos who moved here during the 1990s boom.

Arizona is defiantly different. I think that's why I've always felt at home here. My parents, Wilford and Edna Drinkwine, raised a defiantly different girl.

I was born in California but spent my first ten years living on base at the country's largest Navy munitions depot in Hawthorne, Nevada. My father worked as a civilian there, first as one of the men packing explosives into bomb casings for the war in Germany and Japan and later as a supervisor. For years we were happy—my big brother, Paul, my mom, my dad, and me. We were a close, loving family and were part of a military community that was very much united in the belief that we were part of something noble in fighting fascism in Europe and imperial Japan.

But when I was around eight, my father suddenly got very sick. His respiratory system failed him. The doctors could do little for him other than recommend that he move to Tujunga, California, where the sea air meets the desert to provide an ideal environment, they said, for people with respiratory problems. So we packed up and moved. And when I was eleven, my father died. Losing him devastated our family. No longer a child and not yet a young woman, I was suddenly without the man I had loved most in the world.

What I remember most from this period was the overwhelming grief my family and I shared. But I realize now that my father's death was also my first encounter with the federal government—and it was not a good one.

My father's job had involved years of working around the chemicals and fumes of the munitions plant. All these toxins eventually took their toll and made him ill. I remember how, when he knew the end was coming, he desperately sought government disability and survivor benefits for my brother, my mother, and me. He met and pleaded with our congressman and the Department of the Navy to take care of us. He literally couldn't breathe, and yet he poured every ounce of energy he had left into this final effort. After he died, my mother did the same. I still recall her sitting at the kitchen table with all the paperwork surrounding her, going over facts and dates. And I remember her going, respectfully but persistently, to the congressman's local office to plead for help. But other than a small Social Security check for my brother and me until we were eighteen, no help ever came. For me, it was a painful and important lesson.

My mother had never worked outside the home before. Now she found herself alone with two children to raise. Like all single mothers, she needed something flexible so she could take care of my brother and me. So she took every penny she had and bought a small dress store in Sunland, California. Her reasoning was completely practical: As a small-business woman, she would be the boss. If she had to leave work to be with us, she could. And, of course, we could spend time with her at the store. And that's what we did. She worked seven days a week, fifteen hours a day. She had no choice.

My mother's dress shop became my classroom. The things I learned there, working alongside her during those long afternoons after school, shaped me for life.

For example, I learned from my mother in that dress shop the hard lesson of accountability. When you're the boss, you're the last one to get paid—you get whatever's left after everyone else has their paychecks. I learned patience—and that the customer is always right. I learned initiative. When you're responsible for a business, there's no such thing as a job description. If something falls on the floor, you pick it up. If inventory has to get done, there goes your weekend. No contract, no list of responsibilities defines the limits of your duties. You work until the job gets done. Most of all, I learned not to shrink from a challenge. Running a business is hard work, and it's made no easier by having to raise two children.

I also learned in my mother's dress shop about the power of government and the responsibilities of citizenship. I remember watching her cash out the register drawer at the end of every day. She would separate the sales tax receipts from the rest of the receipts, and it was my job to go to the bank and deposit the money into the two accounts she had created, one for the taxes she owed and another for the rest of the store's expenses. As young as I was, it struck me as odd that there would be two accounts. "It's our money, isn't it?" I asked my mom. And she said, "No, we owe the government." When I asked what for, she said it was for the streets, the firemen, and the schools. She was very patriotic. She said it was everyone's duty to contribute. But I remember detecting a note of apprehension in her voice as well, and I learned later that she kept the taxes separate because she also feared the government: If she didn't have enough to pay her taxes, she knew that she might lose the store.

Like all great teachers, my parents taught me more by what they did than what they said. For instance, when I was very little, my mother was diagnosed with ovarian cancer. She was fortunate and survived with surgery. But I remember that when she came home from the hospital, she was very sick. My father did his best to work and take care of us, but he was overwhelmed.

This was a time when the housing on base was still segregated. But there was an African American family named Johnson that was part of the congregation at our church. God bless them, the Johnsons wanted to help out, so they came to visit us on the "white" side of the base. I remember they brought us food. My dad welcomed them into our home, and my mother, though still very sick, was very appreciative. After they left, our neighbor across the street came over to our house, very upset. He was screaming and yelling about how it was wrong to allow those "niggers" into our home. My father exchanged words with him and—pretty emotionally, as I recall—asked him to leave.

We didn't talk about it again that night. But I vividly remember sitting at my mother's bedside the next day. As usual, the lesson she wanted to impart involved doing the right thing and taking individual responsibility. As she did so many times, she reminded me about the Golden Rule that we needed to live by: to treat others the way we wanted to be treated. She told me the Johnsons were good people, and that it was our home and we could choose to have our friends come to our home. She said our neighbors were judging people by the color of their skin, but that wasn't how I was to judge people. Judge them, she said, by their hearts and by their actions.

My mother's words and, more important, my parents' actions, have stayed with me all these years. I missed my mother more than I can say in those moments after I became governor, when outsiders and critics were saying the most hurtful things about me—saying that I was, in essence, like our neighbor across the street so long ago. If she were with me now, I think she would remind me of her saying: "Doing the right thing almost always means doing the hard thing." I have always strived to do the right thing—for my family, for my state, and for my country. I can't say I've never made mistakes, but I've never backed down from a fight when it came to doing the right thing for the people of Arizona.

My lightbulb moment came at a school board meeting.

I was a young wife and mother, attending a school board meeting in the early 1980s—and I was appalled. I was pretty naive about politics, but I knew a lack of common sense when I heard it, and I heard it when the board members opened their mouths to speak. I went home and asked my husband, John, "Who are those people?" And he said, "Well, they're the school board." So I said, "How did they get there?" He answered, "They were elected by the people in the school district." And I said, "Well, I could do at least as good a job as they are, if not better."

I had been an Arizonan for less than a decade and had never seen myself as a politician. I had married John Brewer, and while he attended school for his chiropractic degree, I worked to support him. When he set up his practice in Glendale in 1970, I was the office manager. And while we were building his business, we were creating a family. We were blessed with three beautiful sons: Ronald, John, and Michael.

I was happy raising a family and putting the lessons I had learned in my mother's dress shop to good use in my husband's business. It was the darn computers that were my undoing. When my husband decided to computerize his business, I took it as my cue to leave. I had never been a technology geek, and I had no intention of starting then. So I went home and started thinking about what to do next. I had to be active. I became a Cub Scout leader. I tried being an entrepreneur with a short-lived jumping-jack (or bounce house, as they are known these days) business. Finally, I got a Corvette for Mother's Day, put on a pair of jeans, and went back to community college.

Then I went to the school board meeting. I wanted to do something to improve education in Arizona, not just for my own sons but for all the kids. I thought they needed some accountability. And it occurred to me, *If I don't do it, who will?* When I told my dazed husband that I was thinking about running for the school board, he gave me some good advice: "Jan, if you really want to have an impact on education, you need to run for the legislature."

That really threw me for a loop. Who was I, to run for the state legislature? How would I go about it? In 1982 there was a new legislative district in the northwest Phoenix area stretching into Sun City that represented a good opportunity for a novice like me. But could I possibly win? I thought about it for three or four days. Then I checked in with John again. I was sitting in the den of our home when he walked in.

> **Me:** Guess what I'm gonna do?
> **John:** What?
> **Me:** I'm going to run for the legislature. I'm going to do it. Will you support me?
> **John:** Absolutely.
> **Me:** [*pausing*] No, I mean *financially*.
> **John:** Oh.

John ended up being my greatest supporter and most valued mentor. But I couldn't rely on him for everything. Running for office meant standing on my own two feet. I had to have confidence in myself before I could ask others to have confidence in me. I found myself, yet again, going back to my mother's dress shop. *If I could have half the courage, independence, and determination that she had*, I thought, *I could actually do this.*

The first order of business was to announce my campaign. I remember sitting in my beach house in Rocky Point, Mexico, hand-addressing invitations asking my friends to join me at my house for an announcement party to kick off the campaign. A few weeks later, more than one hundred people were at my house—even retired Illinois congressman Harold Velde showed up. He turned out to be a huge supporter.

Next I needed to collect enough signatures to get on the ballot.

I had never collected a signature before, and at first I wasn't quite sure where to start. So, like any mom, I started with what I knew best: the grocery store.

Slowly, painfully, I learned how to approach people and ask for their support. More than once, I thought I would give up. But when I finally got up the courage to approach people, I was amazed to find that they would actually sign! After I got my first signature, I couldn't be stopped. "Hi. I'm Jan Brewer, and I'm running for the legislature from District Nineteen. Can I have your support?" I repeated it again and again, with growing confidence. I became a pit bull out there. I actually chased people through the parking lot.

Every morning, to catch the stay-at-home moms while they shopped, I would show up in front of the grocery store—with Ron, John, and Michael in tow—with my tan, my big hair, and my tennis shoes. In the afternoons I would walk door to door in the neighborhoods. And every evening I would be back at the grocery store to corner the people on their way home from work. I did this every day for five straight months.

After I had gathered the absolute maximum number of signatures allowed by law to place my name on the ballot came the real test: fund-raising. This was the part I dreaded most. I couldn't bear the thought of asking people for money. My mother had never taken a dime from anyone—everything we ever had, she earned. The idea of walking up to strangers and asking them to give me money on the promise—even the sincere one—that I deserved their support was completely against my character.

But I was my mother's daughter. I had to do it. So I did it.

I realize now how important it was for me to ask for and receive the donations of those early supporters. I used to have coffees in the backyards of the farmers in my district. We would enjoy the weather, have good things to eat, watch the children run around, and talk about the issues. These people are the salt of the earth. Their beliefs are strong and their desires are simple. They want their families to be safe. They want their families to be provided for. They want to leave behind a better country than the one they inherited. These simple beliefs get twisted and complicated in our political process, but they don't change for the people who hold them. It was important for me, back then, to hear about them firsthand. To get to know the remarkable Arizonans who hold them. To shake their hands and receive their trust and know that it was now up to me to live up to it.

It was at one of these small coffees that I received my first donation. I went to the home of a farmer named Ralph Baskett Jr. I remember taking a few questions from Ralph and his guests and having a nice time. I hoped I had earned their trust and support. And just as I was getting up to go, thinking I had struck out, Ralph left the room for a moment and came back with a check. I was floored. I had received the validation of someone's hardearned money. He trusted me enough to invest in my future. The Baskett family has supported me ever since.

I began my life in public service when I was sworn in as a state representative on January 10, 1983. It was a time of change, both in Arizona and the rest of America. The recession had hit Arizona hard, but the state was changing and growing economically and culturally. When I was sworn in, I was part of the biggest class of female legislators in the country.

In Washington, the Reagan Revolution was under way. It was an exciting time to be entering politics. The country was experiencing a rebirth of freedom, individual initiative, and patriotism. For me, as for so many others, Ronald Reagan was a hero. I looked to him as a bright, steady light of guidance in all the principles that have made our country great.

It didn't take long for this wife and mother turned citizen legislator to start knocking heads for truth and justice. I couldn't help myself. I was constitutionally incapable of backing down when I thought a wrong had been committed. I was surrounded by voices telling me to do the political thing, to think about not upsetting potential supporters in my next election. But those voices were always drowned out by the voice of my mother reminding me that doing the right thing usually means doing the hard thing.

My first brush with controversy set the tone for much of the rest of my career. It was 1985, and I was beginning my second term in the Arizona House. That year, the state was introduced to a genuinely ugly human being: a losing legislative candidate, part-time cabdriver, and full-time publicity hound named Terry Choate.

Think of the Phelpses of the Westboro Baptist Church, that family of psychopaths who hold up offensive signs at veterans' funerals. Terry was just like them, but with less charm.

Terry got it into his head to build a monument to Vietnam War *protesters*. Late in 1985, he bought some land on the west side of Phoenix and applied for permits to create the "Jane Fonda Vietnam Victory Park." He planned to build a thirty-foot tower to fly the flag of Communist North Vietnam, our enemy in the war that had ended just ten years before. He even talked about getting a part of the plane in which Arizona senator John McCain had been shot down to display in the park.

I was chairman of the Select Committee for Veterans' Affairs at the time, and I was hearing every day from outraged veterans. I've always had a soft spot for our veterans, having grown up on a Navy base and known so many families whose fathers and mothers never came back from World War II and the Korean War. I personally thought that what Terry Choate was planning to do bordered on treason. So I decided to shut him down. Over howls of protest from the First Amendment purists, I introduced a bill to outlaw the public flying of the flag of a country with which the United States did not currently have diplomatic relations—in other words, North Vietnam.

In my remarks introducing the bill, it was impossible for me to hide my sense of outrage. Now, when I look at my prepared statement, I can see the righteous indignation written all over it.

The North Vietnamese flag flying over the monument, I told the House, would be "a slap in the face of all our veterans who have fought and those who have died so that we may have freedom! Many came home ZIPPED IN BAGS. For what? For our freedom. And I assure you, THEY DIDN'T LIKE THE WAR EITHER. . . . To allow a communist flag to fly in Arizona is to achieve glory from a traitor's vantage; to dance on the graves of those LOYAL AMERICAN VETERANS who have fought and died for OUR FREEDOM."

I was pretty fired up. To me, this was about much more than Terry Choate. It was about a country that was slowly emerging from years of malaise and starting to feel good about itself for the first time in years. It was about men and women who had sacrificed for their country and come home only to be spat on and called baby killers. Maybe it wasn't fashionable to stand up for these men and women—maybe it wasn't intellectually sophisticated to defend this vision of America—but I really didn't care. I was doing the right thing, as I saw it, for the people of Arizona.

My bill was overwhelmingly approved by my colleagues in the Judiciary Committee but was dropped by the House when it was declared unconstitutional. So I introduced another bill, this one prohibiting the creation of public parks that would be harmful to the public order. At that point a liberal columnist at the *Arizona Republic* wrote a column criticizing my bills (in the most illogical fashion, by the way, equating an America-hating, veteran-insulting professional troublemaker with Dr. Martin Luther King Jr., the Elks club, and even newspaper columnists!).

The columnist's arguments were weak, but the nickname he gave me caught on. It was at this time that Sylvester Stallone's action pic *Rambo: First Blood Part II* was in the theaters, featuring the fighting-for-truth-and-justice character John Rambo. So the *Republic* christened me "Janbo" for my efforts to defend Vietnam veterans. Soon after, S, an editorial cartoonist, drew a cartoon of me with an American-flag bandanna around my big hair, an ammo belt across my chest, and a machine gun slung over my shoulder. From then on, I was no longer just Janice K. Brewer. I had an official nickname: "Janbo."

A couple of years later, after I had been elected to the State Senate, I got involved in another battle that gave me my first real taste of how badly the media can distort issues to suit their agenda. It was 1990, and Tipper Gore, the wife of Tennessee senator Al Gore, was fighting her good fight to warn parents about offensive lyrics on record albums. I had kids who listened to these albums, so I joined her in the trenches. I introduced legislation to require labels on albums with offensive lyrics so that no one under eighteen could buy them in Arizona. This would have an impact on such artists as 2 Live Crew and Ice-T, who were known for their obscene lyrics at the time. Record industry executives vigorously fought my bill. Longtime Arizona resident Alice Cooper lobbied me, and I remember how Donny Osmond, who was trying to toughen his image at the time, flew in from Utah to testify against the bill. He arrived at the committee hearing wearing a black leather jacket and black pants. The committee passed the bill, but I eventually agreed to put it on hold after I came to an agreement with the record industry that they would label albums with explicit lyrics—not just in Arizona but nationwide. So, as far as I was concerned, we had accomplished what we set out to do.

Not, however, without making some enemies in the process. While the legislation was pending, a writer from a small weekly publication in Phoenix began calling me, posing as Doug MacEachern, who was then a reporter from the *Arizona Republic* and today is one of their editorial writers. Under the pretext of talking about the bill, this "reporter" encouraged me to recite some of the offensive lyrics we were complaining about. I should have known better, I guess. But I was not then, and am not now, a distrustful person, and I believed in the cause of safeguarding our kids from this garbage. So I recited the lyrics—including the four-letter words and all of the awful, misogynist things that were polluting our children's minds. The deceitful reporter had secretly recorded our phone conversations, and a couple of days later he showed up at the State Capitol with an 800-watt sound system on a flatbed truck with signs proclaiming, HEAR

JAN BREWER TALK DIRTY! He then blared over the loudspeakers all the four-letter words and horrible lyrics I had read to him. Everyone at the Capitol heard me repeating these lyrics over and over again. It was embarrassing for me, but it was even more embarrassing to the profession of journalism. Classes on journalism ethics started using it as an example of bad, unethical journalism—a wonderful example of why journalists rank below members of Congress in American public opinion surveys.

In 1996, after fourteen years in the legislature, I ran for the Board of Supervisors of Arizona's largest county, Maricopa, where Phoenix is located. Maricopa County was facing bankruptcy and many of my supporters encouraged me to run against the Republican incumbent to get the county turned around. Despite its boring, bureaucratic name, the Maricopa County Board of Supervisors exercises tremendous power and oversight. Maricopa County is bigger than seven states and has a population greater than those of twenty-two states. And when I was elected, the county was in very bad shape. Spending was out of control, and accountability was nonexistent. I'll never forget what *Governing* magazine wrote just before I was elected to the board: "If Phoenix represents the best in local government, Maricopa comes very close to being the worst."

Ouch. So we got to work. I was elected chairman of the board, and under the direction of a very talented county manager, David Smith, we began to make the hard decisions and make changes. We reined in spending. We made elected officials more accountable. We began the process of privatizing the administration of the failing county hospital. By the time I'd ended my tenure on the board, in 2002, Maricopa County's turnaround was so complete that *Governing* came back to take a look. What they saw caused them to do a complete 180. They proclaimed it "one of the two best managed large counties in the nation." Even the *Arizona Republic*, not exactly a cheerleader of mine, called it "one of the most stunning reversals in history [*sic*] of American governance."

For much of America, Arizona's tough immigration law seemed to come out of the blue in 2010. In truth, Arizona has been going it alone for more than a decade, since the fortification of the California and Texas borders pushed the majority of the illegal traffic our way.

By the time I became secretary of state, in 2003, Arizona was fast approaching the crisis point. After easing off a bit following the crackdown after 9/11, illegal entries surged in the middle of the decade. People started to notice the increasingly large groups of men hanging around the post offices and Home Depot stores looking for work. We started to see more and more traffic accidents involving uninsured drivers. Our hospitals began to be overwhelmed with immigrants who lacked insurance but needed medical care. The number of non-English-speaking children in the schools soared. But with the increasing numbers of illegal aliens looking for work there came another type of immigrant. And with these men came the crime, the kidnappings, the drop houses, and the steady loss of Arizonans' basic freedom to live their lives in safety and security.

The federal government wasn't doing its job to secure the border. But while Washington did little to ease the crisis, Arizonans didn't sit still. And it is one of the reasons I love this state so much. We are compassionate, welcoming people. But we knew that if we couldn't count on Washington to enforce the laws, we would.

In 2004, a ballot initiative called Proposition 200 was put before the voters. Prop 200 required individuals to provide proof of citizenship before registering to vote, required voters to provide proper identification at the polls, and required proof of eligibility to receive certain welfare benefits. In other words, only citizens should be voting, and only eligible people who are in our country legally should be receiving welfare benefits. Most of the business community, along with elected officials like Governor Napolitano, Democratic congressman Raúl Grijalva, and Republican senators John McCain and Jon Kyl, opposed the ballot measure. Nonetheless, Arizonans said yes to Proposition 200 by a significant margin. It passed with 56 percent of the vote— including 47 percent of the Latino vote.

I personally supported Prop 200, and as secretary of state I fought legal battles to see it implemented. In doing so, I had to fight not only Democrats like the governor and Attorney General Terry Goddard but some Republicans as well.

For me, the question was simple: As secretary of state, I had dealt with reports of voter fraud involving liberal groups like ACORN (the Association of Community Organizations for Reform Now) paying or fooling illegal aliens to register and vote. And the federal law was crystal clear: Voting is reserved for citizens, either native-born or naturalized. Who else had the right to determine the destiny of Arizona? Of America?

It was my job as secretary of state to implement the voting-eligibility requirements of Prop 200, and I took it very seriously. I knew that the right thing to do was to make sure that no one was denied the right to vote and that no legitimate vote was canceled out by an illegitimate one. So I threw my energies into creating rules to implement the new law. The Department of Justice cleared my new rules, and I moved ahead with implementation. I traveled up and down the state, speaking to civil rights and civic groups, educating people about the new law. Arizona voters had clearly signaled that requiring someone to provide identification to vote—just as we do to board an airplane or purchase liquor—was a legal and reasonable standard.

However, in typical fashion, the Ninth Circuit Court of Appeals intervened just a few weeks before the 2006 election and suspended the requirement to provide proof of identification at the polls. I immediately filed an emergency appeal with the U.S. Supreme Court, which agreed with me and overruled the Ninth Circuit. The Supreme Court said that Arizona had a compelling interest in preserving the integrity of our election process. It was now crystal clear: When you show up to the polls to vote in Arizona, bring your ID. And in the end, through our hard work, we were able to avoid most of the name calling and acrimony that has marked other citizenship initiatives. Just this past June, however, the Ninth Circuit decided to review whether Arizona can require residents to show proof of citizenship when they register to vote. And guess who showed up to oppose us? You guessed it: the Obama administration. They filed a brief opposing our proof-of-citizenship requirement to register to vote, arguing that federal law preempts our state law.

As to Prop 200's final requirement, prohibiting Arizona taxpayer dollars from going toward welfare benefits for illegal aliens, the issue was equally clear. My belief is that, with limited funds available to provide social services, those services should go first and foremost to citizens. Like other states, we have limited resources. And unlike most other states, we are being asked to support a huge, largely poor immigrant population whose presence in our state is due to federal failure. Arizonans made the perfectly reasonable, perfectly moral choice to prioritize their limited resources for their fellow citizens.

In 2007, Arizona followed Prop 200 with the Legal Arizona Workers Act, a law requiring that employers use the verification system E-Verify to ensure that their employees are in the country legally. If they fail to do so, they can lose their business licenses. Here again, Arizona was simply creating new tools to enforce existing federal law. It's a federal crime for employers to employ unauthorized aliens. We all know how poorly this law is honored—and enforced—in most parts of America. Government winks and looks the other way while businesses exploit desperate people and power the magnet that drives illegal immigration.

Arizona could no longer afford to wink at employers who broke the law. So once again, we took matters into our own hands. The legislature passed the Legal Arizona Workers Act, and Democratic governor Janet Napolitano signed it into law. She took some heat for that (I feel your pain!), but, to her credit, she did what she thought was best for Arizona. The usual suspects filed the usual legal challenges, of course. But in the end, the people of Arizona had their voices heard. Earlier this year, the U.S. Supreme Court ruled that federal law does not preempt Arizona's law against hiring illegal immigrants. Arizona can require businesses to use E-Verify and suspend the business licenses of those who hire illegal aliens. By recognizing that states have a right to protect themselves from the effects of the federal government's uncontrolled borders, the Supreme Court's ruling is, I hope, a sign of future rulings to come.

It was a warm Arizona evening in late October 2008 when I received the call that would dramatically change my life.

By then I had given twenty-six years to the service of the people of Arizona. I had changed a lot since I was that shy housewife discovering her inner pit bull in the parking lots of local grocery stores like Bashas', Smitty's, and AJ Bayless back in the early 1980s. I had had some hard knocks, learned some valuable lessons, and had some significant legislative and executive accomplishments. I had run for office eleven times and never lost.

The reason I'd never lost, I think, had to do with the ways I *hadn't* changed in all these years. I still felt very strong ties to the issues and the people who had motivated me back when all I wanted to do was make a difference in my children's education. I felt in many ways just like the citizens I had represented all these years, good people like Ralph Baskett Jr., the farmer who had given me my first campaign contribution. I had always made a point of listening to them to be sure. But I was able to really *hear* them because I had always been one of them. I was that girl in a dress shop, that lady in front of the grocery store. I understood the wants of the people who had put their trust in me and confided in me their desires, their needs, their hardships. God knows I'd had my own.

By the time the phone rang that evening in 2008, I knew the Arizonans I represented, and they knew me. I also knew that my state was in dire fiscal straits. Six years of overspending during the Napolitano administration had had its effect. As a percentage of our general fund, Arizona had the worst budget deficit of any state in the union. To get our state back on track, there was no question that doing the right thing would mean doing the hard things. Tough, unpopular choices would have to be made.

The voice on the end of the phone told me that Governor Napolitano was planning to resign after the coming election to join what was all but certain to be the administration of President Barack Obama. I was temporarily (and uncharacteristically!) speechless. Arizona has an unconventional line of succession in which the secretary of state (that being me at the time) is first in line when the governor can't finish his or her term.

As I grasped the implications of what I was hearing, I almost laughed out loud. As a state senator in the late 1980s and early 1990s, I had fought for a ballot measure to create the position of lieutenant governor to succeed the governor in the case of a vacancy. When our Republican governor, Evan Mecham, was removed from office in 1988, it was our Democratic secretary of state, Rose Mofford, who succeeded him. I felt that the person first in line to succeed the governor should be from the same political party. For six straight years, I fought to create the office of lieutenant governor. It finally made it to the ballot in 1994 for the people to decide. The voters, in their wisdom, rejected the measure.

It was a surreal, bittersweet moment. The Republican nominee for president, John McCain, was my friend. We had started our political careers together back in 1982, when he was first elected to the U.S. House of Representatives and I was elected to the Arizona State House. Now all the indications were that John was going to lose his bid for the White House. But his loss would be my gain. I was going to become the twenty-second governor of the state of Arizona.

CHAPTER THREE

Senate Bill 1070

Janet Napolitano wouldn't leave.

For months there had been speculation that President-elect Barack Obama would appoint her to his cabinet. It only seemed right. She had spent so much time campaigning for him, I barely saw her in the office building we shared at the Capitol. And sure enough, by November the press was reporting that she was Obama's top pick for secretary of Homeland Security. Then, on December 1, President-elect Obama made it official in a televised press conference from Chicago. Governor Napolitano was going to Washington. I was next in line for the governorship. The problem was . . . Janet wouldn't leave.

I was eager to get to work. And there was a lot of work to do. Years of overspending and overpromising by politicians in Phoenix had brought Arizona to the brink of fiscal Armageddon. State government was overspending its revenues by $1.6 billion. I was inheriting the largest budget deficit, on a percentage basis, of any state in the union. Our deficit was even worse than California's!

Governor Napolitano had accepted her post in Washington but insisted she wouldn't resign the governorship until she'd been confirmed by the Senate. So everyone in Arizona sat and waited with frustration. It made no sense that she wouldn't leave. Arizona was in a fiscal mess, but the Republican legislature obviously preferred to wait for their new Republican governor. Signs started to pop up around town that read, JAN BREWER: GOVERNOR-IN-WAITING. Once January arrived, our soon to be ex-governor stuck around to give a lame-duck State of the State speech. She also submitted a budget that would take effect six months after she left. It was a fiscal nightmare, but we had to live with it.

For at least a couple of years, we had known we were heading for a budget disaster. I once told the press that the state simply couldn't afford Governor Napolitano and we'd end up going into bankruptcy if we continued along our current road. I'll admit that the comment was a bit cavalier when I made it. But Governor Napolitano did her level best to make my prediction come true. In four years, she had increased the budget by an unsustainable 56 percent by negotiating large tax cuts in exchange for large increases in spending. Under her watch, the disaster loomed larger and larger, but she took no action to cut spending. By the fall of 2008 the budget had crashed, together with the national economy. Little did I know I'd be the one dealing with the fallout.

As of November 2008, Arizona had an official projected $1.2 billion shortfall in our bloated $9.9 billion budget. Governor Napolitano's last budget was unbalanced and did little to address the looming crisis. She told the press that Arizona was going to be bailed out by the federal government to the tune of $1 billion. "It could be more," she said. And, as she had always done, she doubled down on her fiscal strategy: Her 2009 proposed budget plan had absurd revenue projections and was heavy on borrowing, fund sweeps, and other numbers manipulation. It was light on spending cuts. She suggested Arizona cut just $975 million over 2009 and 2010, even though the combined projected deficit for those years amounted to nearly $4 billion. "[A]s always," she said in her last official address, "there is more to do." More to spend, she meant.

Governor (and she was still governor) Napolitano's confirmation hearings started in mid-January. She left Arizona right after her lame-duck State of the State speech to go to D.C. for the hearings. Although nothing was certain, it looked as though the Senate was going to confirm her immediately after President Obama's inauguration on January 20. That afternoon I had C-SPAN turned on in my office and watched as Senate Majority Leader Harry Reid announced her confirmation. And then I waited. And waited some more. Hours passed, and I finally called Napolitano's staff. "Do you know if she's still resigning today?" I asked. "She was confirmed, you know." Nobody on her staff knew what the game plan was. So we continued sitting around waiting. Finally, at 4:56 P.M., Napolitano's general counsel hand-delivered to me her resignation letter. After weeks of waiting, Arizona now officially had its next governor.

I had to jump right into the fray. I didn't waste time. The next day was my formal inauguration ceremony. In my inaugural address I reminded all Arizonans of the seriousness of the problem we faced:

We find ourselves weighed down with obligation—overdue obligation. We are gathered amid uncertain times, with a difficult work before us. In some ways this feels like you've just shown up for a party—but the guests have all gone, only the caterer is left and she immediately hands you the bill. . . . For decades, the abundance generated by free, hardworking Americans has allowed government to remain in the habit of

*growing, and in recent years to grow even more rapidly. But
today, neither prudence nor our Constitution will allow this to
continue in our state. We have all been seated to preside over
that rarest of political happenings: our government is going to
get smaller. We know this, and so do the people we serve.*

I also couldn't help poking some fun at the new Obama
stimulus package. "[We] are planning a massive stimulus
package of our own, to make Arizona the most economically
vibrant place in the world," I said. "And just like the clever
folks in Washington, we have a catchy name for it: It's called
'freedom.'"

I wasn't joking about freedom. Not at all. I knew as deeply
as I have ever known anything that only freedom could remedy
Arizona's troubles. It has always been American freedom that
has lifted us up in tough times, and it will always be.

I quickly got organized. I didn't have a whole lot of time, and
I didn't have a lot of knowledge about the inner workings of
Governor Napolitano's administration. She'd had me in to the
office only once to visit before I occupied it as governor. But I put
together my transition team. I worked the phones, asking people
to come help me, even if it could only be for a short time. I knew
the kinds of people I needed: Arizonans who knew how to take
charge of a problem and solve it in their own unique down-to-
earth style.

We could still fix the budget, but we'd have to move fast. I
needed to dramatically change the way the state did business,
because the traditional method simply wasn't working. It was
driving us into the ground. In my first official act as governor, I
put a moratorium on all new state rules and regulations. I had

to make sure that Arizona was the most economically vibrant place in the world.

Next I reached out to people who actually knew *how* to do business and begged them to join us in our mission to create the best business environment in the nation. "Government doesn't know how to do business," I said. "Only business knows how to do business, and we need your help in order to overcome the bureaucratic and regulatory climate dominating our state government."

My faith in the Arizona business community was rewarded. Lots of good people left high-paying jobs in the private sector to come help me and the state of Arizona. They made considerable personal sacrifices and had the same desire to turn the state around—a desire to rebuild and reposition Arizona for the next one hundred years.

That didn't mean all of our problems were solved—2009 was a bad year, to say the least, with respect to the budget. I had a plan to fix the budget crisis—I had been down this path before. I thought we had the ability to change things if we did it right. After all, I had changed things in Maricopa County. I had a track record.

I immediately tackled our budget deficit. Ten days after becoming governor, I erased $1.6 billion from our state budget deficit. Education, welfare programs, and public safety took the brunt of the cuts. Even though the cuts were the largest ever in Arizona history, our problems were far from over. We were now facing a $3.4 billion hole for the upcoming fiscal year.

I soon learned that my track record meant very little when it came to getting my supposed allies in the legislature to agree with me. The legislature was Republican, and they were in love with me when I was sworn in. "We've got a Republican!" they said in celebration. They thought I was going to be a rubber stamp for their ideas. They thought I was going to go along with anything they proposed.

They were wrong.

It wasn't long before I started to catch flak from Republicans in the legislature. When I didn't turn out to be a rubber stamp for their plans, they were furious. I vetoed their proposed budgets. I line-item-vetoed certain elements of their bills. This was painful. These were my friends, some of whom I'd known for years. Eventually, down the road, many of them realized that the hard and unpopular decisions I had to make turned out to be the right decisions. I've since received apologies from many of them. But at the time, it was really tough. They were hell-bent to run the show and do things their way. And I was hell-bent on doing things the way I thought was right. They thought we were all philosophically aligned: I'm a conservative Republican, and this was a Republican legislature. But they wanted to tackle everything at once, and they were adamantly opposed to raising any new revenues for the state, regardless of the impact that the budget cuts were having.

Yes, I wanted to cut spending—and I did just that, in historic amounts. But we had to take a hard look at revenues as well. Another $3.4 billion in cuts would be devastating to the areas of education, public safety, and the most vulnerable in our state.

And yes, we also took federal stimulus money. On February 17, President Obama signed the American Recovery and Reinvestment Act of 2009 into law. I was in my car on the way to an interview when Senator Jon Kyl called. "I have good news and I have bad news, Governor," he said. "The bad news is that the president succeeded in passing his stimulus package. The good news is that you're getting a bucketload of money."

"I don't need a bucketload, Senator," I said. "I need *a truckload* of money!" Then I got serious. "Jon," I continued, "we have serious problems. I don't know if we'll get through this."

A few minutes later, during the radio interview, the host told me about other governors who were grandstanding and refusing to accept stimulus funding and asked if I would do the same.

"What, and have the money go to Kentucky?" I asked incredulously. "I won't bite off Arizona's nose to spite her face." In the end, all fifty states took the stimulus money.

Several legislators who publicly proclaimed that we shouldn't take the stimulus funds later begged to have those funds used to save their favorite programs from being cut. For them, it was like their own little cookie jar, but with no accountability for how the cookies got paid for.

I shared many of the legislators' reluctance to put any more burdens on the Arizona taxpayers. I had never voted for a tax increase in my twenty-seven years as an elected official, and I didn't want to start as governor. But our backs were against the wall. Governor Napolitano had run up the deficit and then run out of town—but not before saddling Arizona with another rotten budget plan. I reached out to the best financial experts to go over the books, and they explained to me that they thought historic budget cuts and a temporary tax increase were the only ways to solve our budget problem. The issue we were facing was that we could eliminate all of state government except education, health care, and public safety and still have a massive budget deficit.

I know the majority of Arizonans understood that, as governor, I had to run the government. How were we going to solve this? I pondered these issues for hours, days, weeks. My budget advisers insisted that there was no other way and that I needed to propose a temporary tax increase. I kept coming back to the same conclusion: "I can't do it."

One night, I found myself emotionally spent, sitting on my patio in the middle of the night. It was two or three in the morning, and the desert air was cool. I looked up at the sky. "God, what am I going to do?" I asked. Then I made up my mind: "I'm going to do what is right." For me it always comes back to basic principles. And my mother had told me over and over again that doing the right thing almost always means doing the hard thing. So I steeled myself and whispered, "Jesus, hold my hand. I'm going to do this for the people of Arizona. And if it affects my reelection and my political reputation, it doesn't matter. This isn't about Jan Brewer's political future. It's about Arizona's future."

I went back to work. I told my staff to go back to the drawing board time and time again. I told them that we needed to get our state out of the hole, let the chips fall where they may. The budget we came up with slashed spending and included a temporary one-cent sales tax hike for three years to make up the massive deficit. The sales tax was the fairest method of raising additional revenue, affecting everyone equally, and we calculated that the temporary measure would raise $1 billion a year and protect the areas of education, health care, and public safety from even deeper cuts. Cuts would still be necessary, but this temporary tax would make these cuts less deep.

The voters got it intuitively, I think. They knew me—I had twenty-seven years of credibility as a fiscal conservative. Besides, voters are sensitive to politicians trying to have it both ways.

They can see when politicians are trying to manipulate them to assure their reelection. It ran against my personal political interests to call for the tax hike. A friend of mine, Chuck Coughlin, summed up my position well. "She knew the tax was the only option on the table," he said. "I told her she will have no friends, that not even the Democrats will help you, because they want you to roast in the fire. But she did it."

But the legislature wasn't going to back down, either. They tried to outmaneuver me by passing a budget without the temporary tax, which would have decimated education, health care, and public safety. But then they wouldn't send it to me. They just held on to it. They planned to wait and send it to me on the first day of the next fiscal year, believing I wouldn't veto it and shut down the government. Instead of waiting, I sued them to force them to send me the budget. The Arizona Supreme Court agreed with me, but by the time the legislature actually sent me the budget, it was the early morning of the first day of the new fiscal year. Through careful line-item vetoes and outright vetoes of other budget bills, I avoided a government shutdown. But we still didn't have a finished budget and I immediately called the legislature back into session.

I kept pushing and pushing to get our budget in line. The entire Republican establishment opposed me. Democrats opposed me too, complaining that the proposed temporary tax hike wasn't high enough. My poll numbers began to collapse. By the end of September 2009, my approval rating was down to 37 percent, from 51 percent in May. In potential election matchups, I was being beaten badly by the Democratic attorney general, Terry Goddard.

Republican primary challengers started to come out of the

woodwork—three of them, in fact, including a self-funded millionaire candidate. Great time to announce a reelection campaign, right?

I thought it was, because my principles were on the line. And I was more than willing to put them before the people of Arizona. On November 6, I announced my candidacy for a second term. "When I took office, I inherited a budget deficit created from years of overspending and living beyond our means," I said. "We have worked hard to start fixing this problem, and we have already made and proposed $1 billion in cuts—the largest cuts, my friends, in Arizona's history. Some of these cuts were not easy, but tough times call for a tough leader."

In my announcement speech, I talked about my mother, who taught me the nature of hard work, honesty, and integrity. I talked about how being governor of Arizona was the second-greatest job I'd ever had—being a wife and mother was the greatest—and how I hoped I had made my mother proud. Most of all, I talked about the wonderful people of Arizona, who deserved the best government possible. I concluded by reading a note from John Adams to his wife, Abigail, in which he explained why he felt it necessary to go to Philadelphia to pursue his mission to serve as a delegate in the First Continental Congress. "Great things," he wrote, "are wanted to be done."

"I believe I am the right person to finish the challenging tasks that are ahead of us," I concluded. "And yes, the race ahead of us will be a difficult one. But I intend to win it. I intend to win it because *great things are wanted to be done in Arizona.*"

Those great things could not wait for an election. They had to be done now, regardless of the consequences to my own political future. By February 2010, I was still asking the legislature to either pass the temporary sales tax or put it on the ballot for the voters to decide. I trusted the voters. So I asked the legislature to put the sales tax increase on the May 18, 2010, ballot. They refused, but I kept at it. The crisis was simply too urgent. Finally, after a year of battle, one of the legislators said, "Just give it to her. There's no living with this woman until she gets what she wants."

Finally, I got what I knew was necessary. "At long last, the voters get a voice," I told the *Arizona Republic*. "It is a voice key members of the legislature and I have fought for, a voice for our children and our future, and it was worth the effort. I truly believe that once you give the education to people, and you do the outreach, people will do the math and see there's no other way."

But the fight wasn't over yet. Now the measure had to go to the people of Arizona. I was more than comfortable living with their judgment. But the opposition was out in full force. Many of the legislators actively campaigned against the temporary tax. Both of our senators, John McCain and Jon Kyl, came out against it. I was so politically radioactive that after I complimented Senator McCain during his reelection battle, he said it didn't count as an endorsement. Everyone thought the tax hike proposal was going to kill me. They asked why I couldn't just leave well enough alone, why I needed to carry that political baggage. But I was convinced the voters understood that I was acting in the public interest, that I was doing the right thing, and the tough thing. The polls began to show that I was right. By March 23 my approval numbers had climbed back up to 41 percent. By April 14 I was leading my primary opponents as well as my main Democratic opposition, Attorney General Terry Goddard. The *Arizona Republic* praised my appeal to the public, drawing a simple lesson from my campaign: "Take a strong stand. Connect what they're saying to their own lives and experiences. . . . [Governor Brewer] reeled in listeners by speaking their language, got them thinking, then got out of the way."

Arizonans weren't stupid. They knew that the back-scratching deals between Governor Napolitano and the Republican legislature that had simultaneously cut taxes and raised spending were unsustainable. The politicians had gone home happy and content, sure that their reelections were safe. But the taxpaying citizens of Arizona knew the good times were over.

In the end, the people of Arizona stood with me. On May 18, 2010, the voters came out in droves and supported the ballot measure in a landslide, with 64 percent support. Soon enough, my primary opponents who had been opposed to the measure began dropping out of the race.

I knew my job wasn't done, however. We still needed to cut, and we still needed to streamline government. But I knew—and I still know—that the people of Arizona are practical, wise, and honorable. We don't back off our debts, and we don't shirk responsibility for our spending. We stand together and do the right thing.

Even as we made the hard choices on Arizona's budget, though, another local issue was beginning to seize the imagination of the entire nation.

For those of us who live in Arizona, illegal immigration isn't new. It's not something that happened all of a sudden. Our borders have been open for years, and our state and population have been the chief victims. More than 1,000 illegal aliens come across our border each day.

I had known all of this for a long time. But after I became governor, it became my personal responsibility to deal with it. What's more, illegal immigration into Arizona had changed in the past few years. The drug trade had taken over. Many of the people crossing our border were dangerous, violent criminals. Crime and violence had shot up in our urban areas, particularly in Phoenix. The costs of incarcerating these criminals and providing services to other illegal aliens contributed to a widespread feeling of being under siege. To put it plainly, my job was to protect the people of Arizona. If the federal government refused to do it, I believed, we were going to have to pick up the slack. I wasn't going to allow the crime, the environmental degradation, the lawlessness, and the overwhelming costs of out-of-control illegal immigration to continue on my watch.

I made the executive decision that everywhere I went as governor, I would call on President Obama to do his job—a job that only he could do—to secure our border.

I began a campaign of imploring the feds to help us out. We kept asking for help, begging for help—and they kept turning a deaf ear. Even though Janet Napolitano had spent her time in Arizona fighting the same issues, as a member of the president's cabinet she was now on the other side of the fence, so to speak. We asked them for the money that was owed to us for incarcerating criminal aliens. We asked to be a partner with the federal government, since we couldn't afford to put the National Guard on the border ourselves. Here I was with a broken budget—$3 billion in debt—and I had to deal with a border blown wide-open as though with an invitation: "Y'all come in!"

I had no choice but to put on the pressure. So I began writing letters to the Obama administration. Between March 2009 and

June 2010, I wrote a total of five letters. Not one of them was ever really answered. I received a courtesy reply to my first letter, but the others were ignored entirely.

On March 11, 2009, I wrote a letter to Secretary of Defense Robert Gates, asking for an increased military presence on the border. I wanted at least 250 National Guard soldiers under the mandate and control of the Joint Counter Narco-Terrorism Task Force (JCNTF), using federal funding. "Our citizens must be protected from border violence," I wrote. "Arizona and the other U.S.-Mexico border states continue to be confronted by a number of unique and disproportionate challenges relative to other states and we bear significant reimbursed costs in the public, non-profit and business sectors associated with border related challenges." Secretary Gates never responded.

In April, I joined all of the other border governors—California's Arnold Schwarzenegger, New Mexico's Bill Richardson, and Texas's Rick Perry—to request congressional leadership in putting more National Guard troops on the border. "Securing our border is a critical federal responsibility," we wrote. The response from the Obama administration: nada.

I became like a woman possessed. I called for the feds to "secure our border" until I was blue in the face. At a Senate Homeland Security Committee meeting in Phoenix on southern Arizona border violence, I repeated this call so many times that committee chairman Joseph Lieberman of Connecticut finally said, exasperated, "Governor, we get it. You want your border secure!"

The area where the feds had been the biggest scofflaw, as far as I was concerned, was in failing to reimburse the states for the cost of incarcerating criminal illegal aliens. Like Janet Napolitano before me, I was a broken record when it came to nagging the federal government to pay its share for the 17 percent of our prison population that is here illegally. The Arizona taxpayers pick up a tab of about $150 million every year for this burden. Congress established SCAAP to help the border states defray these costs. The program is always in arrears, though. Governor Napolitano constantly held press conferences berating the Bush administration for her SCAAP dollars with an oversize invoice. When she went to Washington to become Homeland Security secretary, she left behind the invoice prop. We were so desperate, we felt like sending Napolitano her own oversized invoice to get her to send us the money.

Unbelievably, the first year I was governor, President Obama actually cut funding for SCAAP by $400 million. In the midst of his infamous first-year spending spree, he saw fit to underfund an already underfunded federal obligation. To justify the cut, the Obama administration laughably claimed, "In place of SCAAP, the administration proposes a comprehensive border enforcement strategy." This is a lot like a guy at a diner telling the waitress that instead of paying for his lunch, he proposes a global strategy to eliminate world hunger.

That May I finally got the chance to confront President Obama directly. The president was scheduled to give the commencement address at Arizona State University. I met him before he spoke to a packed crowd at Sun Devil Stadium. "I really want to talk to you regarding the dollars that we're owed for the imprisonment of criminal aliens here in Arizona," I said. He was very cool to me. In fact, he blew me off.

As the months went on, all my begging and pleading added up to precisely zero. Not even a "Sorry, we can't help you, Jan!"

or "Try us again next year!" So I did what I had to do. I ordered the state Department of Corrections to return all nonviolent criminal illegal aliens to the custody of U.S. Immigration and Customs Enforcement (ICE). "These inmates are the responsibility of the federal government (as is securing our border with Mexico)," I wrote. "Arizona should not have to bear this cost. . . . The Federal Government is supposed to reimburse local law enforcement for the costs associated with detaining illegal immigrants. Since they refuse to pay their fair share, we will continue to send these inmates to ICE."

On April 6, 2010, I wrote directly to the president of the United States. First I thanked him for designating certain parts of Arizona major disaster areas due to tough winter storms we had had earlier that year. Then I said, "There is yet another emergency facing Arizona, but this one is not the result of a natural disaster. In contrast, this emergency has been the result of decades of neglect and an open unwillingness of the federal government to fully shoulder its constitutional duty to secure our country's southern border with Mexico." Still nothing but radio silence from Washington.

Rob Krentz's murder in March 2010 was the last straw. I remember finally realizing that we could no longer wait for Washington to act during a trip to the border with Representative Gabrielle Giffords just three days after Rob had been killed. We were going to attend the opening of a new U.S. Border Protection facility in Tucson. Tensions were very high. Not just the ranchers, but all of southern Arizona, it seemed, were up in arms over the killing. How we could have allowed this to happen was very much on my mind as I traveled to Tucson to be with Gabby, U.S. Attorney Dennis Burke, and a huge gaggle of media.

While we were there, we met with an official who had been in charge of El Paso's border station and was now in charge of border security in New Mexico, Arizona, and California. I asked him, "What's the difference you see between Arizona and the other places you've worked?" His answer stunned me: "There are no consequences here."

He was exactly right. There are no consequences here. No consequences for crossing the border illegally. No consequences for breaking the law. When the federal government had decided there *would* be consequences to illegally crossing the border in California and Texas, crossings had gone down. But Washington, for whatever reason, had refused to do the same in Arizona, and now Rob Krentz was dead.

Enough was enough. The feds had failed in Washington. Arizonans had to act.

What would become known as SB 1070, or earlier versions of it, had been floating around for years by the time I became governor. National Public Radio would falsely report that the legislation had been hatched in a 2009 meeting between Arizona legislators and representatives of the private prison industry (who presumably, the story noted, would benefit from the law). In fact, Arizona senator Russell Pearce, the original sponsor of the bill, had introduced similar legislation almost every year since 2003.

The bill was the result of a decade of Arizonans watching the federal government take action to secure the border, first in California and then in Texas, but not in our state. Then we watched as Washington tied itself in knots in 2006 and 2007 over immigration. "Comprehensive immigration reform," we knew, was code for perpetuating the failed status quo. We'd been down that road before, and that was no longer an option to consider before securing the border. We found that a lot of Americans agreed with us as we watched even "comprehensive" immigration reform fail in Washington.

By the middle of the decade, after a fivefold increase in the number of illegal aliens in our state and with crime shooting up in our cities, Arizona couldn't wait any longer. Long before SB 1070, we began to address the problem ourselves. We passed Proposition 200 to protect the integrity of our elections and to limit state welfare benefits to those who are eligible. We followed that up in 2007 with our law enforcing the federal law against employing illegal aliens by requiring that employers use E-Verify. SB 1070 was passed in the same spirit as these earlier measures: If the federal government wasn't going to secure the border, we were going to do what we could to make Arizona less attractive to illegal aliens.

The idea is called "attrition through enforcement." What that means is that illegal immigration into the United States can be curtailed—and the number of illegal aliens already here reduced—simply by enforcing the law. The hope was that by creating less of a magnet in the form of jobs and welfare benefits, we would see less illegal immigration to the state. After all, it is Americans and American public officials who are largely responsible for luring illegal aliens to our country in the first place. When you remove the incentives we create through jobs and benefits, you give people less reason to come here illegally. And when you do that, everyone wins. States like Arizona bear less of a burden, and fewer poor, desperate people in Mexico and elsewhere are exploited by smugglers and drug dealers.

SB 1070 continues attrition through enforcement by creating a state penalty for what is already a federal crime: being in the United States illegally. Since 1940, all immigrants have been required under federal law to carry documents showing they are here legally. SB 1070 makes it a misdemeanor in the state of Arizona to fail to carry such documentation. Its language mirrors language found in the federal statute. And contrary to what some of our critics have charged, SB 1070 doesn't permit police to harass people who they think might be illegal immigrants. It allows (but does not require) a law enforcement officer *who is in the course of making a lawful stop* such as a traffic violation to inquire about a person's legal status—but *only if* the individual's behavior and circumstances provide "reasonable suspicion" that the person is here illegally.

This last point bears repeating. Under SB 1070 there are two hurdles a police officer must clear before he can ask someone about his or her immigration status. First, the person must have committed some other violation of the law. Second, the officer must have a reasonable suspicion that the person is illegal. Then, and only then, can the person be questioned about his or her immigration status.

Earlier versions of SB 1070 had passed the Arizona legislature in 2006 and then again in 2008. Despite the fact that she signed Arizona's law enforcing the federal law against employing illegal aliens, then-governor Janet Napolitano vetoed these earlier iterations of SB 1070. But when the latest version of the bill passed the State Senate in February the year after I became governor, I put my staff on the case. I generally don't comment on legislation that hasn't reached my desk, but I knew SB 1070 had the potential to be an important tool in our fight against illegal immigration. I told my staff to work with the legislature, and my instructions were explicit: Any bill I could sign had to meet three basic criteria:

First, it had to work. This was crucial. If it didn't work, the law wouldn't just be pointless, it would be counterproductive. An ineffective law would just continue the political charade. It would be further proof that we weren't serious about stopping illegal immigration. That was the last message I wanted to send.

Second, the bill had to be constitutional—it had to be able to survive the court challenges we knew would come. This was important to me personally, not only because of my deep respect and love for the Constitution and the freedom it preserves but because I didn't want any grounds for a court to strike it down.

Third, and most important, it had to protect civil rights. I was convinced that any law that worked would have to bring Arizonans together, not push them apart. Fears and charges of racism would distract us from the hard work of securing our border and would allow our critics to cast doubt upon our motives. I guess I was naive to think that we could avoid being called racists. Some people, I know now, were going to play the race card no matter how carefully we crafted the law. But it was an overriding concern in the months leading up to the passage of the bill that it equally protect all Arizonans from ethnic profiling and official harassment.

In the midst of our work to refine the bill, Rob Krentz was murdered on the border. It was as if someone had thrown a bucket of gas on a raging fire. A town hall–style meeting with the Border Patrol organized by the Arizona Cattle Growers' Association attracted 350 people to a one-room schoolhouse in Apache, 110 miles southeast of Tucson. The frustration of the community was palpable in the room. One after another, the ranchers took to the microphone to say that they had been warning about something like this happening for years, and for years they had been ignored. There were repeated calls to put the military on the border. One rancher drew thunderous applause when he suggested not only that the military come, but that it be allowed to use deadly force.

Gabby Giffords was Rob's representative in Congress. She joined me and Senators McCain and Kyl in calling for the federal government to act. In a letter to President Obama and Homeland Security secretary Napolitano, Gabby said Rob's killing "is a sober reminder that the safety of U.S. citizens on American soil is under attack. . . . The people I represent are angry and demand action."

Although Napolitano had supported deploying the National Guard to the border when she was governor—and had pleaded with the Bush administration to keep them there in 2008—she refused the calls for action. All the Department of Homeland Security (DHS) saw fit to do was to offer a $25,000 reward for information leading to Rob's killer and to issue an empty statement saying they were "carefully monitoring the situation and will continue to ensure that we are doing everything necessary to keep communities along the Southwest border safe." But clearly their "careful monitoring" had failed. Clearly, what they thought was "everything necessary" was far from enough. We had the grieving Krentz family to remind us of that.

After Rob's death, we ramped up our efforts to perfect the bill so I could sign it. I was still uneasy about how it would be perceived by Hispanics and other minorities. So I had my staff sit down with counsel from community Hispanic organizations to hear their concerns. They walked through the law clause by clause and pointed out the issues they saw with racial profiling and potential rights violations.

I also heard from leaders from the Jewish community and the Anti-Defamation League. These were people I had known for years who were concerned about the impact of the bill on civil rights. I carefully explained all the steps we were taking to make sure no one was treated unfairly under the law because of their race or nationality. I told them that I genuinely believed what I was doing was right for the people of Arizona—otherwise I wouldn't do it.

By the time we were done, we had ironed out many of the problems. In a refrain that would later be picked up and repeated ad nauseam by the national press, critics like President Obama were saying that the bill would allow police to approach people on the street and demand papers for no reason. That was flatly untrue. As we pointed out again and again, the language of the statute created a secondary enforcement regime, which means that there first had to be, to quote the law, a "lawful stop, detention or arrest made by a law enforcement official or a law enforcement agency . . . in the enforcement of any other law or ordinance." In other words, you had to break the law *first*, and only then, if there was "reasonable suspicion" you were illegal, could you be asked for proof of citizenship.

Opponents of the bill also tried to turn the phrase "reasonable suspicion" into something sinister, as though police could profile under the guise of normal discretion. But reasonable suspicion has been a legal standard in use for decades all over the country. No single factor like having dark skin or speaking Spanish counts as reasonable grounds for suspicion. In legalese, a "totality of circumstances" must be present. For instance, we knew as we were working on it that SB 1070 would most often come into play in the context of a traffic stop for speeding or some other common infraction. In that context, for a police officer to form a "reasonable suspicion" that someone in the car is illegal, he or she would have to witness a number of things. Maybe the vehicle is overloaded with passengers. No one has identification to show. The highway they're on is a heavily trafficked smuggling route. Not one single factor but several must be present for the officer to be able to ask for proof of legal residence.

We worked hard to make sure that these criteria were clearly spelled out in the law, but some people insisted on distorting them anyway. Alessandra Soler-Meetz, the executive director of the ACLU of Arizona, claimed that SB 1070 gave "every police agency in Arizona a mandate to harass anyone who looks or sounds foreign." In the end, these arguments came down to nothing more than cheap insults to the men and women of Arizona law enforcement. The presumption seemed to be that underneath their uniforms Arizona's police officers are a bunch of raging bigots who are just itching for an excuse to harass innocent dark-skinned citizens. We've trusted the police to responsibly use the legal standard of reasonable suspicion for decades to fight all kinds of crime. But when we tried to apply the same standard to illegal immigration, suddenly the police were denounced as racists who couldn't be trusted to enforce the law responsibly. I thought it was insulting and disgraceful.

What we also labored to make clear is that SB 1070 doesn't *require* police to stop anyone on the basis of suspicion about illegal status. The law is very clear: Police officers only have to make a "reasonable attempt" to determine immigration status "when practicable." In practical terms, this means that if police are busy with other matters, or believe that questioning someone about their immigration status would be counterproductive, they don't have to pursue it.

The law did some other useful things as well. It prohibited local police agencies from adopting "sanctuary policies" through which law enforcement officials shelter known illegal aliens from possible deportation. It included a ban on hiring day laborers on public streets and public places. It also allowed local residents to sue the state or local government if it adopted or implemented "a policy that limits or restricts the enforcement of federal immigration laws to less than the full extent permitted by federal law."

Most important, we made sure that there was language in SB 1070 that expressly prohibited racial profiling under the statute. The language of the original bill said, "A law enforcement official or agency . . . may not solely consider race, color or national origin" in determining reasonable suspicion. Not good enough. We insisted that the word "solely" be removed so that the bill was unequivocal. We added clear language that police "may not consider race, color or national origin in implementing the requirements of this subsection except to the extent permitted by the United States or Arizona Constitution." The law also expressly states that SB 1070 can only be implemented "in a manner consistent with federal laws regulating immigration, protecting the civil rights of all persons and respecting the privileges and immunities of United States citizens."

At the end of this exhausting process, I truly believed we had accomplished something that would make the people of Arizona proud. But would it be enough to placate those who were waiting to pounce on the bill? I wanted so much to believe that it would be.

I thought we were in pretty good shape. We had a bill that was fair, effective, and most of all would send a powerful message to Washington, D.C. I felt good, but I still had nagging doubts. One night, after a long day of working out last-minute changes, I turned to Richard Bark, my deputy chief of staff for policy, and said, "They're still going to call me a lot of names, aren't they, R.B.?" I could see the pain in Richard's eyes as he admitted the truth. "Yes, Governor, they are," he said. "They are going to call you a racist." Uneasily, I glanced at the floor. "Well," I whispered, "we just can't let them stop us from doing what's right."

The political temperature climbed faster than the mercury in Phoenix as we moved into April. The bill was continuing to move through the legislature, and it seemed as though everyone wanted to know what I was going to do. Phones were ringing and people were screaming. Even former Arizona attorney general Grant Woods, a longtime friend and my campaign co-chairman, was urging me to veto the bill. At our weekly campaign strategy meetings, Grant would lay out his arguments. I always listened respectfully. I wanted to understand people's concerns and fears. Grant didn't change my mind, but he remained co-chairman of my campaign.

As the bill came closer to my desk for signing, more critics came out of the woodwork. Some of the Arizona business community, which had been silent up to that point, suddenly lit up the phones with calls for me to reject the bill. Their talking points sounded like something borrowed from the liberal activist groups. All SB 1070 did was enforce the federal law. What could be their objection to that? Besides, they were coming late to the game. "Where were you during the legislative process?" I asked. They had no answer—no one had shown up. But now that it was time to make a decision, they wanted me to take the heat.

On April 13, the House passed the bill, and the pressure only increased. I still hadn't said publicly whether I would sign it or not, and for a very specific reason. I honestly wanted to listen to people and hear what they had to say. I knew that there are people in Arizona and in the rest of America who don't really believe there should be a border between the United States and Mexico. They don't want the law enforced because they have political, cultural, or commercial reasons to want to ignore it. Some Arizonans, like so many Americans, rely on illegal aliens for cheap lawn care and child care, among other things. Some believed that enforcing the border was enforcing a kind of white privilege—that wanting to control who comes to America was asserting an exceptionalism they do not believe America has. Others, like the labor unions and some in the Democratic Party, see illegal aliens as sources of future votes. As we will see, they believe in open borders as an electoral strategy, plain and simple.

But I knew in my gut that most Arizonans felt differently. And they wanted the law enforced. A Rasmussen poll after I signed SB 1070 showed that 70 percent of Arizona voters favored the bill. I knew the dramatic effect that signing the bill would have, but I also believed it was the right thing to do. There were fifty-, sixty-, seventy-year-old men and women who had lived in southern Arizona their whole lives, and they were living in fear, sleeping with their guns on their nightstands, frightened to go out and walk their dogs or let their kids or grandkids walk to the bus stop alone. This state of fear had to come to an end.

But before I announced my decision, I wanted to hear from as many Arizonans as possible. As luck would have it, the social event of the year for Arizona Hispanics, a fund-raiser for the Arizona Hispanic Chamber of Commerce dubbed the Black & White Ball, was scheduled for April 17, just days after SB 1070 passed the House. It had been on my calendar for a long time. But some of my staff and security detail argued that I should cancel. Tensions were high, and they were increasingly aimed directly at me. My office was being inundated with hate mail, including threats to harm me physically.

I wasn't as worried about my physical safety, but I knew that going to the dinner was a political risk. It could either help my cause or greatly inflame the situation. But I felt the risk was worth it. I wasn't going to hide, and I wasn't going to back down. I owed it to Arizona's Hispanic business leaders. I thought that if I could just explain to them—earnestly and sincerely—that this was a reasonable piece of legislation, maybe I could convince them that we didn't need to have all this tension and protest.

So I went. The media called it my foray "into the lion's den." As we drove up to the hotel, there were protestors outside holding up signs with pictures of Arizona, saying, THE RISE OF THE FOURTH REICH. Tuxedoed attendees had to walk a gantlet of chanting and banging drums. "No justice, no peace! No racist police!" My security detail decided to bring me in the back way. As I walked through the door, I could hear whispers and mur-

murs from the crowd. I thought incredulously, *Some of these people I've known* forever. *Some for forty years! These are my friends. They're part of our community.* I tried to shake it off and made my way to my table.

The ballroom of the Sheraton hotel in downtown Phoenix was packed with Arizona's Latino power brokers. As I sat in the audience, Chamber president Armando Contreras didn't waste time getting to the point. "It is with great respect for you, Governor Brewer, and the office you were sworn to uphold, that I ask that you veto Senate Bill 1070," he said. The crowd responded as if goosed: "Veto! Veto!" Contreras said Latino immigrants were now in danger from a "hostile contingent in our legislature" that made the entire state look "backward and uncaring."

When it was my turn to speak, I got up and addressed the screaming crowd. "In regards to Senate Bill 1070," I said, "I will tell you that I never make comment, like most governors throughout our country, before a bill reaches my desk. But I hear you, and I will assure you that I will do what I believe is the right thing so that everyone is treated fairly." Sensing the opportunity for a cheap shot, Mayor Phil Gordon of Phoenix tried to force my hand: "I think what I just heard was a commitment to veto that bill, whaddya think?" he asked the riled-up crowd. The mayor's goading had its intended effect. More jeers and shouts of "Veto! Veto!" Gordon went on to urge Arizonans to speak out against those who, he said, "would return [Arizona] to the 1950s," when haters hid behind "white sheets."

I walked out proud that I had gone into the lion's den but uncertain as to what I had accomplished. I was listening to my critics. Were they listening to me?

From that point on, the calls rolled in at an unprecedented level, burning up the lines. Phones rang off the hook. During the four-day period from Thursday, April 15, to Monday, April 19, we received more than 13,000 contacts. Just 10 percent of them were in favor of SB 1070.

A few days later, events quickened even further. On Monday, April 19, the State Senate had its final vote on SB 1070, approved it, and transmitted it to me. That started the clock. I had five days to sign or veto the bill, or it would become law without any signature.

Looking back, those five days are a blur of meetings, protests, intensive review of the bill, and profound private reflection. The Arizona Capitol was literally under siege. Protesters had been in the square in front of our copper-domed Capitol for weeks. And from the beginning, it was clear that the protests weren't grassroots—they were Astroturf. The purple T-shirts of the Service Employees International Union (SEIU) were everywhere, as were their professionally printed purple signs that said "SB 1070" with a *Ghostbusters*-style yellow slash through it and the words IT STOPS IN ARIZONA.

That Monday, busloads of chanting, seemingly outraged people began to arrive. The media reported that the unions had brought them in from California, Texas, Colorado, and all over the Southwest. What's more, pickup trucks full of high school kids from Arizona schools began pulling up. Other students walked right out of classrooms and marched over to the Capitol. I guess it was the unions' version of Senior Skip Day. They were chanting, screaming, yelling. They surrounded the Capitol building. At one point, nine students chained themselves to the building, yelling, "Today we are chained to the Capitol, just like our community is chained by this legislation." How exactly their community was being "chained" was left unsaid. Capitol police were forced to cut through the chains and forcibly remove the screaming kids.

Throughout the period before I signed the bill and for months after, the involvement of the unions, particularly the SEIU, in orchestrating protests against the bill was clear. They organized a camera-ready march and rally on May 29 that brought in SEIU executive vice president Eliseo Medina as well as AFL-CIO president Richard Trumka and the co-founder of the United Farm Workers, Dolores Huerta. They descended on Dodger Stadium for the opening game of a three-game series between the Dodgers and the Diamondbacks to protest the bill. Their members filled the stadium to boo Arizona and turn their backs on the Diamondbacks' first pitch. They also demonstrated to put pressure on the Dodgers to stop using their Arizona-based spring training facilities.

As the protests grew, so did the media contingent at the Capitol. The national media descended en masse. Our local stations were joined by ABC, NBC, CBS, Fox, CNN, and MSNBC. What had been an Arizona story—the story of a state fighting back against federal indifference—had become a divisive national issue. All I was trying to do was the right thing for the people of Arizona. But our opponents, particularly the labor unions, seemed to think that the right thing for us was the wrong thing for them. They were determined to rally their base—and inflame the passions of Hispanics all over the country—by twisting and distorting what was happening. They issued calls for a massive campaign of nonviolent "civil disobedience all over Arizona and all over the United States of America."

And sure enough, protests against SB 1070—a bill with the force of law only in Arizona—broke out in cities from Los Angeles to New York. What exactly were they afraid of? We weren't sure. All we knew was that they were virtually inciting riots, and the national media couldn't get enough of it. As I sat in my office on the ninth floor, I could see helicopters hovering overhead like giant dragonflies. My security detail became so concerned for the safety of state employees that SWAT teams took up positions on the roofs of the Capitol and executive buildings.

Even before the bill had been signed, liberal activists, abetted by the national mainstream media, were moving into boycott mode. The *New York Times* said we'd gone "off the deep end," and the *Los Angeles Times* suggested that our state was "hostile." They had said none of this when Janet Napolitano signed measures designed to curb illegal immigration, and had seemed totally unconcerned about the rising levels of violence on the border. But their campaign of distortions and lies was already having an effect. "I am notifying you that I will never be able to visit Arizona again," one misinformed citizen wrote. "[SB 1070] reminds me so much of Germany in the 1930s and also Communist Russia. . . . There is a real sense of hatred in your state now." We received scores of notes like these. I wish I had had time to write back to these folks and let them know they'd been lied to. In the end, very few people made good on these threats, but at the time it was unbelievably frustrating.

While the pandemonium grew outside the Capitol, my staff and I pored over the bill. We had already spent a lot of time working to shape the law, but I wanted—I needed—to make sure that every *i* was dotted and every *t* was crossed. I got our policy wonks together for hours on end, with me grilling them and ensuring that I understood every provision down to the marrow. I went through it as carefully as humanly possible to make sure it was exactly what we wanted it to be. I was still worried, however. "We have this nice thing on paper here," I said. "But we all know that too often things written on paper don't translate into real life."

The clock was ticking on the five days I had to make my decision, but I asked my staff to go back to the drawing board. I was still deeply concerned about perceptions that the bill was racist, even though I knew it wasn't. We know there *are* racists out there, but we also know that our police officers are the finest men and women our state has to offer. They're professionals. So we began crafting a solution: an executive order mandating training of the police on how to implement SB 1070 in a nondiscriminatory manner. Later, I would use the same pen I used to sign SB 1070 to sign an executive order requiring that every peace officer in the state be trained in the provisions of the law and specifically forbidding racial profiling.

I also wanted to highlight our belief that, while SB 1070 was an important tool in discouraging illegal immigration, it wasn't the solution to our problems. So I had my staff put together a detailed plan of action for securing the border. My plan asked for more covert National Guard reconnaissance, aerial patrolling, military exercises along the border, more support for local law enforcement, and improved county and federal interaction with regard to border security. I announced the plan on Thursday morning, April 22, the day before the law had to be signed. The media largely ignored it. It was, after all, a realistic, detailed plan to solve the problem. Where was the story in that?

On March 27, 2010, both respected Arizona rancher, Rob Krentz, and his dog, Blue, were killed on the Krentz Ranch in southern Arizona. Rob paid the ultimate sacrifice for the federal government's negligence in credibly securing the border. *(Courtesy of Sue Krentz)*

Three days after Rob Krentz's death, I attended the opening of a new U.S. Border Protection facility in Tucson, which had been on my calendar for months. At the opening, Representative Gabrielle Giffords and I talked about Rob's death and how we needed to get the border secured and protect the ranchers and their families. *(Courtesy of the state of Arizona)*

It's estimated that each illegal alien who crosses Arizona's border leaves along the way six to eight pounds of trash in the desert. *(Courtesy of the state of Arizona)*

ABOVE AND TOP RIGHT: I was born in California but spent the first ten years of my life living on base at the country's largest Navy munitions depot in Hawthorne, Nevada. My father worked as a civilian there, first as one of the men packing explosives into bomb casings for the war in Germany and Japan, and later as a supervisor. Years of breathing in the chemicals and fumes of the munitions plant eventually took their toll on my father, and he passed away when I was eleven. *(Courtesy of the author)*

After my father died, my mother took on the task of raising me and my brother, Paul. I missed my mother more than I can say in those difficult moments after I became governor. If she were with me now, I know she would tell me to follow the Golden Rule, and she'd remind me, "Doing the right thing almost always means doing the hard thing." *(Courtesy of the author)*

On December 1, 2008, Governor Janet Napolitano and I formally certified the November election results. Earlier that day in Chicago, President-elect Barack Obama had introduced Arizona governor Napolitano as his choice for secretary of the Department of Homeland Security. The waiting game for Napolitano to resign began on this day. (*Scott Cancelosi*)

When President Obama came to Arizona State University on May 13, 2009, to deliver the commencement speech, I asked him why he wanted to cut Arizona's funding for incarcerating criminal aliens. The federal government owes Arizona over $880 million. The president just blew me off and walked away. (*Michael Brewer*)

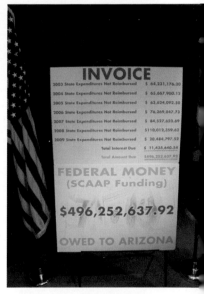

When Janet Napolitano went to Washington, D.C., she left me this giant oversize invoice she had created for President Bush. The invoice is how much the federal government owes Arizona for incarcerating criminal aliens. I thought about sending this to her to remind her that the invoice is still past due. (*Michael Brewer*)

On the day I signed SB 1070, this protester proudly waved the Mexican flag in front of the Arizona State Capitol while draping the American flag around his body. (*Scott Cancelosi*)

Banners like this, with swastikas and calling Arizona a racist state, were commonplace at the State Capitol after I signed SB 1070 into law.
(Michael Brewer)

While marching against SB 1070 in front of the Arizona State Capitol, a protester carried this uniquely intertwined Mexican and United States flag.
(Michael Brewer)

I'm taking my last phone call before leaving the Capitol to sign SB 1070. In the office with me are my chief of staff, Eileen Klein, and my director of legislative affairs, Scott Smith. We're listening to Grant Woods, my campaign co-chair, who wanted me to veto the bill.
(Joseph Kanefield)

LEFT: On April 23, 2010, I signed SB 1070. I believe Arizona, like America, is governed by laws. Respect for the rule of law means respect for every law. *(Michael Brewer)*

BELOW: After I signed SB 1070, protesters placed large banners out on the grass in front of the State Capitol depicting me in a Nazi uniform and calling me Hitler's daughter. *(Michael Brewer)*

Linda Eddy, an artist in Iowa, created a poster of me as Rosie the Riveter, the icon for women working on the home front during World War II. The image went viral on the Internet after I signed SB 1070. *(Image by Linda Eddy)*

Soon after the poster of me as Rosie the Riveter went viral on the Internet, look-alikes would dress up and appear at my speeches to give extra support. *(Michael Brewer)*

After I signed SB 1070, flowers, gifts, and cards poured into my office from across the country. Many gifts were handcrafted, such as this gourd, which was meticulously carved, hand-painted, and personally delivered to my office by a California resident. *(Michael Brewer)*

After meeting with President Obama in the Oval Office on July 3, 2010, I walked outside the White House to address the press. My deputy director of communications, Kim Sabow, had warned me there was *a lot* of press. I was completely surrounded! *(Joseph Kanefield)*

I'm standing with Bas Aja, the executive vice president of the Arizona Cattle Feeders' Association, as we listen to Sarah Palin declare, "We are all Arizonans now!" Governor Palin was a fearless ally as she stood with me demanding that the federal government secure the border. *(Michael Brewer)*

Greta Van Susteren from Fox News has interviewed me several times regarding SB 1070 and securing the Arizona border. In this interview on June 16, 2010, Greta came to Arizona and interviewed me in the desert. *(Courtesy of the author)*

The federal government has posted these signs in our Arizona desert warning Arizonans to stay away from their own land! The sign above *(right)* showed up in our desert—and eighty miles away from the border—two weeks after I met with President Obama in the Oval Office. *(Ryan Smith)*

On January 11, 2011, I visited the victims of the Tucson shooting at the University Medical Center. After spending time with Gabrielle Giffords's husband, Mark Kelly, and her mother, I visited the growing memorial outside the hospital. I brought a bouquet of flowers and took a moment to stop and pray for all the victims. *(Courtesy of the state of Arizona)*

On February 11, 2011, I countersued the federal government for failing to secure our border. I announced the countersuit to catcalls and jeers from these protesters outside the federal courthouse. *(Michael Brewer)*

On May 2, 2011, I'm sitting as Border Patrol agents escort the family of fallen agent Brian Terry to the Peace Officer Memorial. Agent Terry was killed in the Arizona desert in December 2010. Two guns from the ATF's Operation Fast and Furious were found near Agent Terry. *(Michael Brewer)*

Throughout those five days, the pressure mounted. I was taking fire from the unions, some Hispanic groups, liberal special interests—even some of my supposed allies on the right. The United Farm Workers sent me a note that utterly misread the bill and insisted that racial profiling would be the inevitable side effect. "Will an undocumented immigrant from Ireland be a suspect?" they asked. "Probably not. Will Latino dads bringing their sons to spring training baseball camp be suspects? Perhaps. Will the thousands of farm workers who harvest our food be automatic suspects? Certainly." This was a gross and purposeful misreading of the law. The law did not require police officers to interrogate Latino visitors—in fact, it banned them from doing so on the basis of race.

The U.S. Hispanic Chamber of Commerce followed suit. Apparently, walking into the lion's den at the Black & White Ball hadn't won me any points. The chamber declared that the bill would "jeopardize the safety of Arizona communities and result in the racial profiling of Latinos." Even more hurtful was chamber president Javier Palomarez's suggestion that by signing the bill I would be "attacking the entire Hispanic community in the zeal for enforcing civil immigration laws."

I had been working on amendments to the bill since March, including a trailer bill that would make improvements to SB 1070. Even as I worked to get the bill in shape, I began receiving flak from conservatives asking why it was taking me so long. Some people claimed that I was waiting for a poll to come out before making up my mind. One of my opponents in the Republican primary claimed that he would have signed the bill on the first day. The fact that I was receiving criticism from both sides actually made me feel *better* about taking the extra time.

But any feeling of reassurance that week was short-lived. The waterboarding continued. The evening before I had to make the call, I was slated to appear at a dinner for Chicanos por la Causa, a group formed in 1967 to advocate for Arizona's Mexican American population. It promised to be another one of my "into the lion's den" moments. Earlier in the week, Chicanos por la Causa had sent me a letter stating that SB 1070 would "force entire communities to live in perpetual fear of harassment." This was intemperate, to say the least, and highly uninformed. It certainly didn't promise a smooth reception that night. Once again, some of my staff suggested that I cancel. But I insisted on attending. I wasn't ashamed of what I was going to do. But I knew that if I didn't show up, they'd think I was, or that I didn't have the courage of my convictions. I wasn't going to run and hide.

On the way to the downtown Sheraton that night, I could feel the tension in the air. There were the by-now-familiar mobs with their by-now-familiar signs. I found out later that the group protesting was something called the Coalition for Humane Immigrant Rights of Los Angeles—they had bused the protesters in from California! Once inside, though, things were quieter. I could see that there were Arizonans there who didn't agree with me but wanted to be respectful and hear me out.

And then there were those who didn't. Erica Gonzalez-Melendez, the chairwoman of the board for Chicanos por la Causa, rose with the supposed purpose of introducing me. But after a perfunctory reading of my résumé, she launched into a diatribe. She gave up any pretense of addressing the crowd and spoke to me directly. "The eyes of our state and the eyes of the nation are upon you. What sits before you on your desk is the most painful piece of legislation directed at Latinos in the recent history of our state," she publicly lectured me. There were raucous shouts and applause. "We are the people whose sons and daughters have fought greatly for this nation. People who've buried their sons, their heroes, in this soil. Now, as you consider signing a bill that makes those same people second-class citizens," she continued, "Governor, we want to remind you that we vote too. Governor, we ask—actually, we respectfully demand—that you veto Senate Bill 1070." There were screams of applause. There was a standing ovation.

"Embarrassing" doesn't do it justice. Every word of this speech was insulting, even slanderous. The law I was about to sign didn't turn anyone into a second-class citizen. It didn't target vulnerable communities or give racist police a license to harass innocent workers and defenseless kids. It was an act of deep respect for the people of Arizona—people of all races—who'd fought and died to defend our freedoms and our rights.

This isn't an attempt to have an adult conversation, I thought. It was just nasty.

When I finally took the microphone, I talked, as I had many times in the past, about my mother and how she taught me that a person is measured by how she meets challenges. Since the moment I became governor, I said, I had been confronted with the challenge of how to keep Arizonans safe and prosperous. I told the crowd that I had thought about this challenge and prayed about this challenge. "I am my mother's daughter," I said. "I am up to the challenge." I wasn't yet ready to announce whether I would sign SB 1070, but I wanted them to know that I would do what was right for Arizona, regardless of whether or not it was popular.

Then I thought—being Pollyanna again—that I would try to address their concerns. They were yelling questions: "Are you going to veto it? What are you going to do?" So I said I'd take a couple of questions. I got into a dialogue, trying to calm the place down a little bit, to let them know I wasn't their enemy. Even as I spoke, I could hear the catcalls. As I left the stage, the crowd chanted, "Veto! Veto! Veto the bill! Veto the bill!"

By that point, the crowd was openly hostile. *This is pointless,* I thought, *and counterproductive.* As I got up to leave, things got truly out of control. Shouting and screaming broke out. My security detail had to surround me to get me out through the back door. Fearing that I was physically under threat, they had to slam the door on the crowd. Outside, there was a huge group with signs of me dressed in Nazi attire alongside Joe Arpaio, our famously tough sheriff—and a supporter of the bill— sporting a Hitler mustache. A reporter from a free weekly paper chased after me and asked how it felt to be "America's number-one racist." He was from the same paper that had pulled the record-labeling stunt on me twenty years earlier. I had learned my lesson about dealing with this paper a long time ago. I just kept walking.

I learned later that even after I had left the room, the shots kept coming. One particularly cheap one came from a familiar source, Phoenix mayor Phil Gordon. "I have to believe in your heart that you don't want to be a puppet governor whose strings are being pulled by the likes of Russell Pearce and Joe Arpaio," said Gordon.

"I understand your plight," Mayor Gordon said condescendingly, as though I were still in the room. "It's an election year.

You're facing a tough Republican primary and you love your job. I ask you to love your state even more."

I left thinking the whole evening had been a wasted opportunity. There had been no dialogue, only grandstanding and demagoguery. No one had seemed interested in solving Arizona's actual problems, only in scoring political points. One such group was the SEIU. They cut a video of the chanting protestors, exhorting their members to sign a petition on their Web site to veto the bill.

Later that night, the police estimated that 1,200 people—many, like the protesters at the dinner, bused in from other states—had amassed to protest at the Capitol. Several hundred stayed into the night and held a candlelight vigil. Apparently the cheap shots and grandstanding designed to inflame an already combustible situation had paid off. I hoped they were pleased with their night's destructive work.

The morning of Friday, April 23, dawned overcast. Over the course of the day, it would get warm but still pleasant; by afternoon it would be in the seventies—a perfect day for a demonstration at the Arizona Capitol. As we made our last-minute preparations inside, the police estimated that 1,500 protesters—some for the bill, most against—had gathered outside. It was the most intense and violent day of protests yet. About eighty officers were called in to control the crowds. One supporter of the bill was surrounded by angry opponents, and police had to escort him away. Fights broke out and water bottles were thrown. Officers had to separate the two sides with police tape and, at one point, a human chain along West Jefferson Street, to the south.

Supporters were corralled into the courtyard between the House and Senate buildings. Opponents, it seemed, were everywhere else.

Watching uneasily from inside, I knew what I was going to do. I knew what I *had* to do. We had taken a lot of time to sign the bill. That was because we wanted to vet it down to the ground. During that time, friends I had known for years had called me, some begging me not to sign the bill, some equally adamant that I support it. These were people I respected, people whose counsel I had sought in the past. As a leader and a citizen, I owed the public the opportunity to have as much input in the process as possible. And between the letters, the phone calls, and the e-mails, I was listening to the people and giving them the chance to convince me that I was wrong. Nobody did.

It's always tough when people who are close to you passionately disagree with you. A couple of friends got personal, implying that I was a racist. It really hurt to hear that. Of course, I realize now that I was probably naive. I had wanted so much for this to work, and I was no doubt foolish to think that I could convince my opponents of my serious and honorable intentions. But after all, I thought, they knew me. They had elected and reelected me for decades. I had never been called a racist before. The signs and catcalls were very uncivil. You think you can ignore it or hide it away in a dark corner of your brain, but when you get ready for bed at night and say your prayers, that's what's in your mind.

Truly, only my faith helped get me through that trying time. I prayed for God's guidance and support. "Please, dear God," I prayed, "give me the strength to do what's right." I believe in the power of prayer, and there were people in my office who prayed with me. For that I couldn't be more grateful.

I remember one particularly emotional phone call during this period. Someone called me, nearly weeping on the phone. "Governor, have you considered what Jesus would do?" he asked. That one I could answer emphatically. "I can assure you that that is at the forefront of my thoughts," I said. "That is one of the first things I considered."

At 11:42 A.M., I announced that we would hold a press conference at 1:30 P.M. to make public my decision. Because of security concerns, we decided to move the press conference to an Arizona Department of Transportation building, a couple of blocks from the Capitol. It was the only place where my team could create a controlled environment. It was also the only location where we could accommodate all the media. Students immediately walked out of their classes and gathered at the Capitol to protest—hundreds of them, skipping school with the tacit or active approval of their teachers.

The hours passed slowly. The atmosphere in the office was very emotional. At around noon, one of my staffers visited the Capitol and took pictures of the crowd hanging me in effigy. I was very tense. The whole situation was eerie. We could hear all the chaos going on outside.

At about the same time, my son Michael came into my office. He had been out watching the protesters. Michael hadn't seen me in a while, and he knew this was one of the most difficult days of my life, so he came bounding into my office with a big grin on his face, just to try to buck me up.

But I was in no mood. "Wipe that smile off your face," I snarled. "Today is *not* a good day."

I look back on that now with horror. Here was someone coming to give me support—and not just someone, but my son! And I said that to him. I instantly felt terrible for it. But thankfully, Michael stayed by my side throughout the fight. He understood why I was cranky with everything that was happening. All I wanted to do was the right thing for the people of Arizona. That was all I'd set out to do; that was all I wanted. But trying to solve a crisis that my state hadn't created and wasn't responsible for had led to this.

When we finally left the building to drive to the press conference, we saw just how ugly everything had turned. What really infuriated me was the defacing of the American flags. People were stomping on them and writing things on them. Meanwhile, Mexican flags were being waved in the air. Protesters were waving these foreign flags, chanting, "This is our country—it belongs to us!" I heard later that Mexican television was carrying spoofs depicting me as a racist. On their version of the *Today* show, they had a male actor dressed up like me. He asked people for their "papers" and Tasered people who couldn't produce them.

Finally, it was time.

It was a major media event. Stations across Arizona interrupted their programs. Channel 9 in Tucson broke into *One Life to Live* to cover the press conference. CNN carried it live to the nation. They were calling it the "moment of truth." At 1:30, I strode to the podium. Behind me stood rows of police officers. Some were in uniforms but most were in civilian clothes, because their political superiors wouldn't be seen supporting the bill. But I wanted them there, because I wanted people in Arizona and across the United States to see the officers who would be enforcing the law—not some nameless, shapeless, militaristic arm of the state government but the brave and decent men and women tasked with implementing SB 1070.

After I thanked everyone for being there, I moved over from the lectern to a small desk to sign the bill. As I sat down, however, I realized that I had forgotten my glasses on the lectern. Even at the most consequential moments, reality intrudes. I stood up again, laughing at myself on the inside, held up a finger to ask the press to wait just a second, grabbed the glasses, and sat back down. Then I signed the bill.

As I returned to the lectern, I took time to thank the members of Arizona law enforcement who had joined me that day. They were the heroes who were going to have to implement the law, and also the ones who were going to meet with the closest scrutiny—as they should. I sighed deeply, collected myself, and addressed my fellow citizens—and the country.

"We must acknowledge the truth: People across America are watching Arizona, seeing how we implement this law, ready to jump on even the slightest misstep," I said. "Some of those people from outside our state have an interest in seeing us fail. They will wait for a single slip-up, one mistake, and then they will work day and night to create headlines and get the face time they so desperately covet. We cannot give them that chance."

I promised to prove the alarmists and the cynics wrong by enforcing the new law evenly and without regard to skin color, accent, or social status. I promised to make all Arizonans proud. I finished by quoting Teddy Roosevelt: "No man is above the law, and no man is below it." I promised to make good on my heartfelt conviction that Arizona, like America, must be governed by its laws.

It didn't take five minutes for my idealistic hope that I could avoid being called a racist for endorsing the rule of law in Arizona to be proved wrong. After a few substantive questions from the press, one reporter asked, "What does an illegal immigrant look like?" I couldn't help laughing ruefully. They wanted me to profile, I guess. "I do not know," I answered truthfully. "I do not know what an illegal immigrant looks like."

A few minutes later, after I had left the press conference, I found out that earlier that day, at a ceremony in the Rose Garden, President Obama himself had attacked Arizona and SB 1070. "Our failure to act responsibly at the federal level will only open the door to irresponsibility by others," he said. While acknowledging the culpability of the federal government, he issued no call to correct this failure in an appropriate way and simply poured fuel on the fire, asserting that our law "threaten[ed] basic notions of fairness that we cherish as Americans."

President Obama's administration had done nothing—*nothing*—to work with us to secure the border. In fact, his administration had ignored our requests for help again and again. Now he was acting as though none of that had ever happened, and that the real problem wasn't federal inaction but state *action* to protect the people.

I'd never heard of a president weighing in on whether a governor should sign or veto a state bill, let alone one that neither he nor (as it turned out) his attorney general had bothered to read, and I had no idea he'd made those comments when I signed the bill. If I had, I would have responded publicly by telling the president that all he had to do was start enforcing federal law, as we'd pleaded with him to do over and over again.

I was exhausted and triumphant, but I was also filled with foreboding. For good reason, as I was soon to find out.

CHAPTER FOUR

Nazis in the Desert

Declaring that "the states will take the lead, and Arizona will take the lead among states," an Arizona governor signs sweeping legislation enforcing federal law regarding illegal aliens. She calls it "the most aggressive action in the country," explaining that "it is now abundantly clear that Congress finds itself incapable of coping with the comprehensive immigration reforms our country needs."

"Because of Congress's failure to act," the governor says, "states like Arizona have no choice but to take strong action to discourage the further flow of illegal immigration through our borders." Her critics erupt. They file lawsuits, one of which ends up with the Supreme Court. Protests spring up throughout Arizona. Work stoppages and strikes break out.

Before I go further, let me note that the governor in question isn't me. It was Janet Napolitano, who in 2007 gave the go-ahead to the Arizona Legal Workers Act, designed to crack down on illegal immigration by imposing sanctions on businesses that violate federal law by hiring illegal aliens.

The reason you're reading about SB 1070 right now and not about the Arizona Legal Workers Act is simple: With his reaction to the law, President Obama made SB 1070 a national issue. When Governor Napolitano signed the Arizona Legal Workers Act, President George W. Bush never mentioned it. He didn't stir the pot. President Obama did.

Before I signed SB 1070, President Obama had already condemned it as irresponsible and unfair. In the days that followed, he upped the ante. Eric Holder, his attorney general, stated immediately that the Department of Justice would look into whether it should sue Arizona to stop implementation of the law. Janet Napolitano, ensconced in her new role at Homeland Security, hypocritically remarked that she had "some deep concerns with the law . . . it will detract from and siphon resources that we need to concentrate on those in the country illegally, those who have committed the most serious crimes."

If the president and his cabinet officers couldn't stop themselves from encouraging mass hysteria over the law, you can imagine the situation on the ground in Arizona. While President Obama was claiming, with virtually no evidence, that Hispanics were going to have their privacy systematically invaded, his political allies, without a trace of irony, were gathering around my home to protest.

Huge buses from Texas and California began driving up to my front yard; we had reports that the SEIU was sponsoring the tactic. The first time the protesters showed up, I didn't have any security. I had to call them in, but I did so only after one of my advisers told me I couldn't go outside. Soon the radical antiwar group Code Pink showed up too. They set up their lawn chairs on the sidewalk of my ordinary suburban neighborhood, sang, and burned candles. They were relatively respectful—at least, as respectful as people staking out your house to pressure you can be. They never crossed into my yard, but they did cross into my neighbors' yard—they're Puerto Rican and Mexican American, by the way—and, boy, were the neighbors ticked off!

It had gotten to the point that people thought my house—my

personal home—was fair game. We had to station the Department of Public Safety, our state police, there. It seemed unnatural to have guards outside my home. As a legislator, I was used to having Arizonans come up to my house and knock on the door and come on in with their comments and concerns. But that era was clearly over. In the community, many of my friends were concerned about my safety. "Be careful," they said. "We've got your back." I brushed those kinds of comments off—how bad could things get? But I wasn't really grasping the volatility of the situation. I started getting death threats. One kid with an intellectual disability in the Midwest—who thought he was helping me out—even tried to put a bounty on my head.

I'd say the tone for all this hysteria was set not just by the president—although he could have done a lot to tamp it down—but by the tragically misinformed and hyperbolic response of Cardinal Roger Mahoney, archbishop of Los Angeles. The cardinal was the first high-profile figure to play the Hitler card. Unfortunately, he would not be the last. The day before the legislature sent the bill to me—before I had announced whether I would sign it or not—Cardinal Mahoney wrote, "I can't imagine Arizonans now reverting to German Nazi and Russian Communist techniques whereby people are required to turn one another in to the authorities on any suspicion of documentation." *Are you kidding me?* I thought. There was no provision in the bill for anything like that. Where did he get this crazy idea? He continued, "Are children supposed to call 911 because one parent does not have proper papers? Are family members and neighbors now supposed to spy on one another, create total distrust across neighborhoods and communities, and report people because of suspicions based upon appearance?"

These comments poured gas on the flames. It was grossly irresponsible. But I understood why he'd done what he had done. As archbishop of one of the largest Hispanic populations in the country, he probably felt that he had to rap Arizona on the knuckles for defending herself, especially because of the way SB 1070 had been misrepresented by the president and in the press. But comparing Arizona to Nazi Germany, or Russia under Stalin? Who writes this stuff? Do liberals really believe these insane comparisons?

Unfortunately, instead of being laughed at in the press or appropriately shamed by more responsible public figures into toning down their rhetoric, opponents of the bill kept on playing the Hitler card. Eventually, it became a common sight. It was as if there were an underground printing press somewhere, churning out Nazi-themed placards and slogans. One night after the bill was passed, I was leaving the Capitol when I saw a large banner spread out on the grass in front of the building. I asked my security detail to stop so I could take a look. The banner showed me in a Nazi uniform. HITLER'S DAUGHTER? it blared. SHE CLASSIFIES PEOPLE BY WHERE THEY WERE BORN. HISTORY REPEATS ITSELF. IF ARE [sic] NOT BLONDE AND HAVE BLUE EYES . . . BE AWARE! Later I heard reports of the same banner showing up at a protest in Dallas.

And on it went. The rap group Public Enemy's Chuck D recorded a song called "Tear Down That Wall" and told *Billboard* magazine that he had done so because "the governor is a Hitler." I wondered whether Chuck D knew that Communists, not Nazis, had built the Berlin Wall. But never mind. Colorado representative Jared Polis said the situation was "reminiscent of second-class status of Jews in Germany prior to World War II, when they had to have their papers with them at all times and were subject to routine inspections."

California Democratic congresswoman Linda Sánchez actually said that white supremacist groups had been the motivating force behind SB 1070. "It's been documented," she claimed, without offering a shred of proof to back up her ridiculous assertion. "It's not mainstream politics. . . . It creates a Jim Crow system where based on the color of your skin you could be treated as a second-class citizen or harassed based on how you look." Not to be outdone, a New Jersey newspaper published an editorial cartoon showing Hitler with an Arizona-shaped mustache. You had to give them points for creativity.

The low point came on April 26, our first day back at work after the signing. Statehouse employees coming in early that morning found refried beans smeared on the doors of the legislative buildings in the shape of swastikas. The gourmet vandal had written on the sidewalk, AZ=NAZI. It was the first case of hate-crime vandalism—and it had taken only forty-eight hours.

It got so bad that even the Anti-Defamation League, whose Arizona regional board chair had accused the law of "engendering fear, encouraging discrimination and fanning the flames of hatred," came out and publicly condemned the Hitler comparisons. "No matter how odious, bigoted, biased and unconstitutional Arizona's new law may be," said the ADL's national director, Abe Foxman—leaving no doubt as to his own position on the bill—"let's be clear that there is no comparison between the situation facing immigrants, legal or illegal, in Arizona and what happened in the Holocaust."

•   •   •

My biggest mistake was reading the blogs. I knew I shouldn't have done it. But I couldn't help myself. I had a Google alert on my name, so every time "Jan Brewer" showed up on a blog or in a news story, I would get an e-mail. There were the usual comparisons of me with Hitler and the Nazi references. (I was beginning to notice that there wasn't a lot of original thinking among my critics.) I was called a "brainless blond bimbo." My family was mocked. My education was mocked. Even my church was mocked! One particularly articulate writer wrote, "F—YOU JAN BREWER YOU F—ING RACIST BITCH!!!!!!!!!!!! F—YOU AND THE NAZI FACISTS WHO SUPPORT YOU YOU OLD F—ING HAG!"

It was tough, but toughest to take were the comments aimed at Arizona. I read how the state I love was being called "Nazizona." People inside and outside the state were wishing the worst things on my state, starting with boycotts and ending with acts of violence.

Reading comments like these tore me apart and confused my heart and my brain. How could people say such things? How could they even think them? Was there really so much hatred out there in the country at large? Is this to be the reward for any public servant who tries to do the right thing, even—especially—when it's the hard thing? When you spend midnight to five o'clock in the morning reading nasty things about yourself, your husband, your children, and your friends, you begin to question your judgment. I couldn't help wondering whether I had done the right thing after all.

My staff yelled at me to stop. "Don't go near it!" Chuck Coughlin, my political campaign consultant, told me. "You know who these people are? They're losers. They don't have a life! They're sitting there with no shoes on, bare-chested, drinking a beer and smoking a cigarette. They hate the world!"

What saved me were the supporters I heard from: ordinary men and women, not bosses of any union or shills for any liberal interest group—just everyday Americans who shared my commitment to civil discourse and the rule of law. On Facebook, I quickly developed thousands of friends who did not hesitate to take on the haters. One person would post something ugly and there would be a dozen people ready to respond. When I first set up my Facebook page (Facebook.com/GovJanBrewer), it took us six months to get to 2,000 friends, and when we did, we were excited. By the Monday after signing SB 1070, it had jumped to 10,000. From there it grew exponentially. As I write, I have almost 500,000 friends on Facebook, and every day I take time to read the comments people leave on my wall.

Support also came in through other channels. As soon as I signed the bill, I started receiving letters from people around the country saying thank you. Newell Orr, vice president of the Sun Lakes Republican Club, wrote an encouraging note: "Thank you for sticking to your guns and keeping your word. . . . We appreciate you even though the 'Messiah' attacked you today. A lot of people out here back you 100%." Another supporter wrote me a moving note: "For the sake of our country, someone has shown the courage to confront the issue. This will spark progress on a national level." Letters like that were the wind beneath my wings. I thought, *Okay, the people get it. The people understand.*

A couple of days after I signed the law, my chief of staff, Eileen Klein, and my deputy chief of staff for policy, Richard Bark, saw a couple get on the elevator in the Capitol. The couple didn't look as if they worked in the building. They were carrying this beautiful platform with a meticulously hand-carved, painted gourd on it. It depicted a majestic eagle carrying the U.S. and Arizona flags along with the words Freedom to Choose. They had made the whole thing by hand. They lived in California but had driven to Phoenix to personally deliver it to my office.

A few days later, a blanket arrived at the office, crocheted by hand. It was accompanied by a card. The handwriting was shaky—it was pretty clear that it had been written by an older person. The note explained that she couldn't afford to send the blanket but that she had wanted to give me some comfort, so her neighbors had agreed to pay for the shipping.

In another gratifying moment, I was campaigning in Bullhead City when I was approached by a man I found out later was a Vietnam veteran. He was a big guy, a rough-looking character. To look at him, you wouldn't think he was necessarily all that concerned with politics, so I wasn't sure why he wanted to speak to me. Did I mention that it's hot—very hot—in Bullhead City? My makeup was melting, and he wasn't exactly cool as a cucumber, either. He walked right up to me, put his arms around me, and gave me a big, sweaty hug. "I am so thankful to you and proud of you for what you've done," he said. "I fought for our country, and now you're fighting for our country. We believe in you. Don't let us down." Tears were streaming down his face. What do you say when someone says that to you? I was so humbled. I was almost—almost!—left speechless by his support.

It was those kinds of things that got me through the days— things like that hug from a veteran in Bullhead City whose name I never knew. They helped to renew my conviction that I was doing what was right for Arizona. In contrast to the noisy, hate-filled rhetoric and orchestrated protests from the left, I'm still amazed at the quiet gestures of support I received from private citizens all over the country: the letters, the flowers, the gift baskets, the artwork, the cards, the flags, the woodworking, the hundreds of personalized T-shirts, handmade pens, books, carvings, angels, and scripture. I received so many flowers from across the country that my office looked like the neighborhood florist shop. I love flowers, so I thought it was wonderful!

I was more gratified by these gestures of support than I can say. But still, I was worried. The media and special interest reaction to the bill had been at once intensely negative and outrageously misinformed. Could the people see that what I was doing was the right thing? The answer came the Tuesday after I signed the bill, when a Rasmussen Poll showed that an amazing 70 percent of Arizonans supported SB 1070, while an astounding 60 percent of all Americans said they would support a similar law. Despite the constant and deliberate campaign of distortion, it was a tremendous relief to know that a clear majority of Americans was on our side.

One of the most entertaining expressions of this support came a few weeks later when an artist in Iowa, Linda Eddy, created a poster of me as Rosie the Riveter, the iconic image of the women who worked on the home front during World War II. The cartoon image showed me in a blue work shirt with my sleeves rolled up and a red polka-dot bandanna on my head. I'm flexing my muscles next to the words ARIZONA: DOING THE JOB THE FEDS WON'T DO! As soon as Linda released it on her Web site, LindaEddy.com, the cartoon went viral on the Internet. (Yes, the Internet can also be a force for good!) It was even made into T-shirts, buttons, coffee mugs, and bumper stickers. I was so flattered. It was a perfect expression of the strength of our state and the optimism we felt about its future. Most important, it reflected the message we had tried so hard to get across: We were doing the job that the feds wouldn't do. It was wonderful to know that so many Americans got it.

Just as state employees in Phoenix were arriving to swastikas painted in refried beans on the Capitol doors, in Washington the Obama administration was getting to work as well—seeking to undermine the law and thwart the political will of Arizonans.

On *Good Morning America* that Monday morning, Homeland Security secretary Janet Napolitano sounded off about SB 1070. The law, she pronounced, was "misguided." Viewing the issue through the peculiarly distorting lens of a federal bureaucrat, she complained that because we wanted to enforce federal law, we were going to inspire other states to imitate us, creating a "patchwork" of laws and throwing the country into chaos. Good heavens, we can't have too much of that messy local democracy, with people in different states just doing what they want. Of course, this is precisely what she herself had done only a couple of years earlier. It was further proof of the adage "Where you stand depends on where you sit."

But give Janet credit for toeing the party line—she knew what her boss wanted to hear. And the very next day, President Obama reinserted himself into the debate over our state law. At a fund-raiser in Ottumwa, Iowa, he reached new heights of distortion in describing the adverse impact of the law. "Now suddenly if you don't have your papers and you took your kid out to get ice cream, you're going to be harassed—that's something that could potentially happen," he said. This was a ridiculous and totally irresponsible assertion. In fact, it was a total inversion of the law. For a police officer to ask a law-abiding family on an innocuous errand like buying ice cream about their immigration status would be a *violation* of SB 1070, not a consequence of it. I watched the coverage of the president's remarks in my office in the Capitol and fumed. There was no way this kind of misinformation could be anything but a deliberate attempt to inflame people's passions and stir up opposition to the bill—a textbook case of demagoguery.

The leader of the free world wasn't the only head of state who was cynically twisting the argument. Immediately after the law was passed, the Mexican Foreign Affairs Ministry issued a travel advisory to Mexicans traveling in Arizona. This was apparently their response to the U.S. State Department's repeated advisories to Americans traveling in Mexico because of the hideous drug cartels and violence in that country. I guess they thought it was tit for tat. Only we hadn't kidnapped or beheaded anybody; we had just passed a law.

A few weeks later, Mexican president Felipe Calderón came to Washington for a state visit. Standing next to President Obama on the south lawn of the White House, the Mexican president took aim at SB 1070, and both leaders showed their clear disdain for the law.

> **President Obama:** In the United States of America, no *law-abiding person—be they an American citizen, illegal immigrant, or a visitor or tourist from Mexico*—should ever be subject to suspicion simply because of what they look like. [Emphasis mine.]

> **President Calderón:** We will retain our firm rejection to *criminalized migration* so that people that work and provide

things to this nation would be *treated as criminals*. [Emphasis mine.]

I couldn't believe what I was hearing. Put aside the misrepresentations of the law in both of these statements; both leaders were simply rejecting the idea that there was anything wrong with crossing the border illegally. They were openly disregarding the law and rejecting the very existence of the border. And they were standing there, in the safety of the White House compound, calling those who wanted to enforce the law not just wrong or misguided. They were calling us racist.

It got worse the next day when President Calderón addressed a joint session of Congress. There, he proceeded to lecture Americans about SB 1070. "I strongly disagree with your recently adopted law in Arizona. That's why I agree with the president that the law carries a great amount of risk to the values we both care about," Calderón announced as Democrats in Congress rose and cheered. "It is a law that not only ignores a reality that cannot be erased by decree but also introduces a terrible idea using racial—racial profiling as the basis for law enforcement."

I was apoplectic. Racial profiling? Calderón clearly didn't understand what the law actually said. And why should he, when the president of the United States—a former law professor—was saying the same thing! Had he even read the bill? And what hypocrisy! Calderón was pointing the finger at us when, in fact, Mexican laws regarding illegal immigration to his country are essentially the same. In Mexico, local police are required to check the immigration documents of people they suspect are not in the country legally. The difference is, in Mexico many of the police are more likely to beat and rob illegal aliens than deport them. Human rights groups report that police routinely racially profile migrants and have been involved in kidnappings of migrants. We had honest police and had built safeguards against racial profiling into our law. Where did Calderón get off?

For Harry Reid and Nancy Pelosi to give the president of Mexico a global forum to malign the state of Arizona and its duly enacted laws was nothing short of outrageous. As I sat there and watched, I had to wonder where our country was going under Obama. It started to dawn on me that this president and his liberal allies in Congress don't really understand what America is all about and what our fundamental principles are. We are the greatest country in the world, yet he was acting as though *we* were the problem. Americans, he seemed to be saying, rarely live up to their principles and therefore must learn from those who would victimize us. This wasn't hope and change; this was recrimination and blame.

It was then that I knew that we were in a war. My staff and I had worked hard over the past four months, putting in long days, agonizing over every detail, debating with our critics and ourselves, to craft a law that would be effective and fair. We had been scrupulous about mirroring the federal law: If SB 1070 was racial profiling in the state of Arizona, then the federal government had been racially profiling for decades. We had gone beyond the letter of the law to see that our officers were properly trained. I had done everything I could in the naive hope that I could avoid having my motives impugned for doing what was necessary to protect and serve the people of my state.

None of it had mattered. As I listened to the American and Mexican presidents lecture Arizonans on political morality and "fairness," I was suddenly reminded of the bitter statement Rob

Krentz's family had made about how nothing ever changed down on the border because of political forces "on both sides of the border." I knew then that they were right: There was an agenda at work that didn't want the law enforced. After oil exports, money sent home from Mexican immigrants living in America is Mexico's chief source of foreign income. President Calderón clearly wanted to keep the gravy train coming and to look tough for the cameras back home to boot. As for President Obama, it seemed as though the only thing he liked better than the status quo of uncontrolled illegal immigration was having the target of SB 1070 to shoot at. By accusing us of being bigots, he could look as if he were doing something about immigration when he was actually doing nothing at all.

Supporters of this agenda would always play the race card to get their way, because that was the most powerful weapon in any debate. There is nothing worse than being called a racist in America today. It demonizes those it describes and makes their views unworthy of discussion or debate. What is the point of trying to have an adult conversation with a racist? Opponents of SB 1070, from the president on down, were throwing this accusation around so frequently not because they wanted to fix the border but *because they did not.*

I was involved in a war with a deeper and more entrenched set of political interests than I had realized. But at least, thank the Lord, I wasn't alone. The cavalry came charging to the rescue in the form of Sarah Palin, beaming in via satellite from Wasilla. While talking with Sean Hannity on Fox News, she promptly put the rhetorical wood to President Obama. "Governor Jan

Brewer did what she had to do as the CEO of that state," Sarah said in her inimitable style. "To help protect the citizens of her state, she had to do what the federal government has refused to do, and that is help secure the border."

Governor Palin also brilliantly analyzed President Obama's failure to respect or understand the Tenth Amendment—the one that reserves to the states all powers not specifically granted to Congress. The president had ignored the Tenth Amendment when it came to Obamacare by mandating that citizens purchase a good that they have a right not to buy. By the same token, Palin said, Obama would neither allow the states to enforce federal law nor enforce it himself. He wanted it both ways: states as powerless lackeys of the federal government, and states as powerless non-lackeys of the federal government. Arizona's new law, she said, was "telling the federal government that they better wake up, buck up, and do their job in securing our borders."

Throughout the battle that was to come, Governor Palin would be an insightful and fearless ally. She rallied Americans to stand together and declare, "We're all Arizonans now." She goaded the president to do his job, observing tartly that "Jan Brewer had the cojones that our president does not have." I will forever be grateful for her courage in standing with me in this fight.

I did some fighting back myself that week as well. The day after Sarah first spoke about SB 1070, I took to the airwaves to defend myself and my state. During an interview on Fox News with Greta Van Susteren, I explained, "We have no other choice. We have a right to feel free in our state and feel safe." Greta asked whether I had spoken with Secretary Napolitano. "She obviously is turning a blind eye to Arizona. She understands what the situation is," I replied. "For her to make the comment that she made that—what was it?—that the borders are more secure than they've ever been, well, they've never been secure." Finally, I told Greta what I had realized listening to Presidents Obama and Calderón: This wasn't a debate about securing the border. It was a Democratic vote-getting scheme.

The president's ill-judged comments had lit a fire that would soon consume the state of Arizona. Prominent figures began calling for a boycott of the entire state in retaliation for having exercised our constitutional and God-given rights to defend life, liberty, and property. Believe it or not, one of the first to call for a boycott was one of our own congressmen. Even before the bill was signed, Democratic representative Raúl Grijalva went on Keith Olbermann's show and called on private businesses to hold their conventions elsewhere. It was a move he would come to regret.

The union for Major League Baseball players was another of the first to jump on the bandwagon. A statement issued by the Major League Baseball Players Association (MLBPA) on April 30 reflected all the disinformation and propaganda about the law that was being spread by its critics. The statement expressed concern about the law's effect on foreign-born athletes playing on Arizona teams. Any international player, it read, "must be ready to prove, at any time, his identity and the legality of his being in Arizona to any state or local official with suspicion of his immigration status. This law also may affect players who are U.S. citizens but are suspected by law enforcement of being of foreign descent." It was the same old inaccurate tune: Racial profiling would somehow inevitably be the result of a law that explicitly *banned* racial profiling. Why? Because Arizona law enforcement could not be trusted to carry it out fairly. This baseless and insulting allegation was rarely stated but was plainly the hidden subtext of the debate.

The MLBPA's statement led directly to an attempt by liberals to move the All-Star Game from Arizona. Mike Lupica, a renowned sports columnist for the New York *Daily News*, wrote that if SB 1070 was allowed to go into effect, "Major League Baseball ought to announce that a sport in which 30% of the players are Hispanic will not hold the 2011 All-Star Game at Chase Field in Phoenix." Mike Freeman, a columnist for CBSSports.com, suggested that under the new law the following scenario could take place: "It's 2011 and the All-Star Game is just a few days away in Arizona. Albert Pujols decides to take a stroll in downtown Phoenix. A police officer drives by and doesn't realize that Pujols is a baseball icon. To the officer, he looks potentially like an illegal alien. He is, after all, brown skinned. Pujols is stopped by the police. 'Papers please,' the officer says. If Pujols somehow forgot to bring proof he's an American citizen on his walk, then potentially off to jail he'd go." This guy had clearly seen too many movies in which menacing Gestapo agents demand to see a terrified refugee's papers. What's more, it was the president's own doing, the thrust of his own arguments, channeled through the mouths of sportswriters all over the country.

Professional basketball, too, cranked up the liberal propaganda machine. And what made it even worse was that my favorite basketball team, the Phoenix Suns, hastened to jump on the bandwagon. Managing partner Robert Sarver decided the team would wear their "Los Suns" jerseys on Cinco de Mayo for

Game 2 of the Western Conference Semifinals as a gesture of solidarity with Arizona's Hispanic population, which was purportedly under attack. General Manager Steve Kerr even played the Hitler card, saying, "It's hard to imagine in this country that we have to produce papers. It brings up images of Nazi Germany." The media loved this stunt and broadcast images of the defiant players in their Los Suns jerseys far and wide.

What they didn't report was that the jerseys had been created as part of the NBA's "Noche Latina" marketing campaign, aimed at attracting more Latino fans. The team had worn the jerseys back in March, before anyone outside of Arizona had ever heard of SB 1070. So when Sarver and Kerr saw the opportunity to strike a fashionable political pose *and* promote their marketing campaign, they passed it off as a bold stand on moral principle. Some two-fer!

A few weeks later, the boycott movement gained more steam when the Los Angeles City Council, which can't even handle issues in L.A., voted 13–1 to boycott Arizona businesses. I appreciated Councilman Greig Smith's lone "no" vote. But many council members used the opportunity to pander to their Hispanic constituents, who they assumed would be strongly opposed to the enforcement of our borders. "An immigrant city, an international city, [Los Angeles] needs to have its voice heard," intoned Councilman Ed Reyes. "It is crucial this great city take a stand." San Diego, Oakland, and San Francisco joined Los Angeles in voting for boycott resolutions or condemning the law.

When I heard about the L.A. council vote, I couldn't help but be slightly bemused. "I find it really interesting that we have people out there that are attempting a boycott in favor of illegal actions in Arizona," I told the press. "That to me is just unbelievable." Meanwhile, Al Sharpton showed up right on schedule—always eager to find a camera and microphone willing to follow him around. "The Civil War is over," Sharpton said. "Let's not start it again with states' rights."

This is another of the left's favorite ploys, along with the race and Hitler cards. Because southern segregationists invoked states' rights to resist desegregration, the left has claimed ever since that any appeal to the principle of federalism is code for racism. Linking SB 1070 with slavery and segregation in this way wasn't just insulting, it was disgusting.

Some people may have canceled their vacation plans in Arizona as a result of this campaign. (Jerry Brown initially made some noises about doing so, but after his election as California governor, he came to Arizona anyway.) In the end, the state wasn't greatly affected by the movement. Moreover, it never did seem to dawn on the boycott's supporters that the people who would be most hurt by it were precisely the less well off, Spanish-speaking Arizonans they were allegedly trying to help.

Based on some often-repeated stories of convention cancellations, the mainstream media and liberals continue to push the idea that SB 1070 has devastated Arizona tourism. While there was some impact on the convention side of tourism, annual visitations to Arizona were up by an estimated 4.5 percent from 2009 to 2010. And the boycott didn't only work one way. People began traveling to Arizona just to show their support.

People who are unfamiliar with the Arizona desert tend to think of it as something out of *Lawrence of Arabia*: hot and lifeless. In fact, there's a lot of life in the desert. And the temperature can swing wildly, falling from over 100 degrees in the daytime to the 50s at night. The desert is an unpredictable place.

So is Arizona politics, as President Obama soon found out.

It began at the White House Correspondents' Dinner, that see-and-be-seen Washington social event that attracts self-important Hollywood celebrities to a rubber-chicken dinner with journalists and politicos. On May 1, President Obama spoke at the event, which is traditionally supposed to be a laugh-fest, with some self-effacing humor and good-natured political banter. That's the idea anyway. But about halfway through his speech, the president turned his shtick into an attack on Arizona. "Unfortunately," he said to the chuckling crowd, "John McCain couldn't make it. Recently he claimed that he had never identified himself as a maverick. And we all know what happens in Arizona when you don't have ID." He paused and added, his voice dripping with scorn, *"Adios, amigos!"*

I don't know about people in the rest of the country, but Arizonans found the president's joke offensive and not funny. He and the rest of the Washington crowd didn't seem to take illegal immigration seriously—except when they were fishing for votes. We thought they should know that we didn't appreciate this lame attempt at humor. So we made a YouTube video to put his comments in their proper context.

To a background of ominous music, the video recites the grim facts of illegal immigration in Arizona: organized criminal drug gangs, rampant kidnappings, prosecutors unable to keep up with a crushing load of drug cases. Funny stuff!

"So what does President Obama have to say about Arizona doing the job Washington won't?" the video asks. It then cuts to President Obama's joke at the Correspondents' Dinner, with liberal champion Alec Baldwin grinning ear to ear in the audience. "President Obama," it concludes, "broken borders *are not* a laughing matter."

The final frame: "No one in Arizona is laughing. Do your job and secure the border."

The video was a real morale booster. More than a million people have viewed it—thousands in the first days alone. It was at that point, as I recall, that we felt the tide begin to turn. Slowly, bit by bit, truth and reason staged a comeback against the organized disinformation campaign that had been waged against SB 1070.

Another positive sign was the backlash that had built against the Los Suns basketball jersey stunt. The mainstream media loved the story, but the fans didn't. Many were outraged that the team would take such a political stand, and they let the owners know on talk radio and online. A group of season ticket holders made their own statement by showing up at a game sporting T-shirts that read VIVA LOS 1070. They were told by the management that they had to turn their shirts inside out. When they refused, security guards tried to throw them out of the arena. But they were able to return to their seats after appealing to the Suns' security director. The shirts became so popular that one of the original guys told me he had to spend all of his time shipping them out to meet the demand. He sent me one.

Then, on May 13, baseball commissioner Bud Selig did the right thing by ignoring the calls for a boycott. He met with team owners and purposefully steered clear of the issue. Instead he focused on baseball's efforts to reach out to minorities. "We're a social institution," Selig averred. "We've done everything we should do. It's our responsibility. We're privileged to do it. And we'll continue to do it. That's the issue and that's the answer." If he had still owned the Milwaukee Brewers, they would have become my second-favorite team on the spot.

Hearts and minds were being changed—if they had ever really believed the lies they were told to begin with. But the real game changer came from an unlikely source: the Obama administration.

Someone once said that what's called a gaffe in Washington is really just a politician inadvertently telling the truth. Attorney General Eric Holder had been bad-mouthing SB 1070 from the beginning. In a high-profile appearance on NBC's *Meet the Press* on May 9, Holder pronounced that SB 1070 "has the possibility of leading to racial profiling" and said that the Justice Department was thinking of filing a lawsuit. Then, just four days later, came the attorney general's moment of inadvertent truth. In testimony before the House Judiciary Committee, Holder admitted that he hadn't even read the bill he'd been bashing for almost a month. Here's how the truth came out in Holder's remarkable exchange with Congressman Ted Poe of Texas:

> **Representative Poe:** So Arizona, since the federal government totally fails to secure the border, desperately then passed laws to protect its own people. The law is supported by 70 percent of the people in Arizona, 60 percent of all Americans, and 50 percent of all Hispanics, according to the *Wall Street Journal*/NBC poll done just this week. And I understand that you may file a lawsuit against the law. Seems to me the administration ought to be enforcing border security and immigration laws and not challenge them, and that the administration is on the wrong side of the American people. Have you read the Arizona law?
> **Attorney General Holder:** I have not had a chance to; I've glanced at it. I have not read it.

Poe: It's ten pages. It's a lot shorter than the health-care bill, which was 2,000 pages long. I'll give you my copy of it if you would like to have a copy. Even though you haven't read the law, do you have an opinion as to whether it's constitutional?

Holder: I have not really, I have not been briefed yet.

That hadn't stopped him from roundly condemning it, though.

In the attorney general's defense, he did say later in the hearing that he was basing his opinion of SB 1070 on "things I've been able to glean by reading newspaper accounts" and "obviously, looking at television." Given the amount of disinformation that had been "reported" about the law in the mainstream media, it's perhaps understandable that the attorney general formed the opinion he did. I just think the nation's chief law enforcement officer should consult something other than *The Rachel Maddow Show* before pronouncing judgment on a statute duly passed by the elected representatives of the people of Arizona. Maybe I'm being picky.

But that wasn't all. It was about to get worse for the Obama administration.

A few days later, State Department spokesman P. J. Crowley, after equating the Arizona law with the tyranny of the Communist Chinese, admitted on national television that he hadn't read the bill, either.

Then, just a few days after that, Homeland Security secretary Janet Napolitano admitted that even she hadn't read the bill—even though she had until quite recently been governor of the state of Arizona. She had called the bill "misguided" virtually hours after it was passed. But when she was questioned by a congressional committee, she had to admit, "I have not reviewed it in detail. I certainly know of it," she added lamely, trying to get herself off the hook. Then she stated, "That's not the kind of law I would have signed. . . . It's a bad law enforcement law."

Watching it all from Phoenix, where the Capitol was still under siege, I was dumbfounded. Here were the two most important law enforcement officials in the country and the spokesperson for the State Department, all criticizing the law in public forums while admitting that they had not bothered to read it!

Despite the grief and aggravation all of this caused for us, Paul Benz, from my very creative campaign staff, found a way to somehow make us all laugh. He shot an ad featuring a Kermit-like frog puppet conducting a sing-along for kids. Over a bouncy sound track, he sings: "Reading is really super swell. Reading's great so let's all shout out loud! Reading helps you know what you're talking about. Let's see what these folks have to say about reading." Then the video cuts to Holder, Crowley, and Napolitano, all admitting that they hadn't read the law.

"Kermit" looks flummoxed. "Seriously?" he says, before walking offstage in disgust. It's an amazingly lighthearted take on the tragedy of the Obama White House's response to the immigration crisis. It's well worth Googling "Arizona Sing-a-Long."

The ad made us laugh, but we *had* to laugh to keep from crying. We had a raging brush fire in Arizona—one that was starting to leap across state lines and ignite the entire country—and instead of trying to contain and put it out, our leaders in Washington were throwing gas on it.

"A nation without borders is like a house without walls," I said solemnly. "It collapses. And that is what is going to happen to our wonderful America. And we can start the turnaround here in Arizona. That's what we intend to do. We are not going to stop. Mr. President and Secretary Napolitano, it is your responsibility to secure our borders, and I plead with you and I ask you respectfully: Do your job."

I was on Fox News again with Greta, giving my pitch for what felt like the millionth time. The president and his administration weren't hearing me. But the American public was. My state, our law, and I personally had been subject to an incredible onslaught of criticism and vicious attacks. Individuals who, for whatever reason, didn't know or care how my state was suffering from unrestricted illegal immigration or how the crisis was spreading elsewhere had attacked us with fervor, but Americans still stood with me. A Fox News poll taken after the law was passed found that 61 percent of American voters thought that Arizona had been right to take action rather than wait for the federal government. What's more, 64 percent of people believed that the Obama administration should wait and see how the law worked rather than take action to stop it before it was implemented.

President Obama could read polls too, and he clearly didn't like what he was seeing. He never called me. We never talked. But we soon found out—on the radio, just like everybody else— that he was deploying 1,200 more National Guard troops to the border to protect us against the Mexican cartels. He was also asking Congress to okay $500 million for more border protection and law enforcement. I gave credit where credit was due. "My signing of Senate Bill 1070 has clearly ignited the talk of action in Washington for the people of Arizona and other border states," I said in a statement. "I am pleased that President

Obama has now, apparently, agreed that our nation must secure the border to address rampant border violence and illegal immigration without other preconditions, such as passage of 'comprehensive immigration reform.'"

I then asked President Obama to do more. "Success will be determined by facts on the ground, not by the size of unfulfilled promises of rhetorical flurries. I am anxious to hear of the details that have not yet been disclosed of where, how, and for how long additional forces will be deployed." Words were great, I was saying, but now it was time for action, and this action just wasn't enough. The 1,200 additional guardsmen were less than half of what we needed. The month before President Obama's announcement, Senators Kyl and McCain had asked for 3,000 more National Guard troops.

Don't misunderstand me. I was glad that the president was at least making a gesture toward stronger enforcement. But our needs were much greater than that, and a token gesture of this kind wouldn't really begin to address them. Not only that, but President Obama had several times now singled out a state law—our law, a law I had signed—as a threat to American civil liberties. *And he and I had never discussed the issue.* My letters had gone unanswered, my requests for a meeting ignored. Maybe he didn't want to talk to me. Maybe I was more useful to him as a bogeyman than as a public policy partner. I didn't really care. I believed that the people of my state deserved the attention of the world's most powerful man, if only for a few minutes. What was happening to us was too important. What was coming for the rest of the country was too serious. I was determined to take my case directly to the president.

What is the saying—When God closes a door, he opens a window? Well, my window turned out to be something called the Council of Governors. President Obama himself had appointed me to the group to coordinate on issues of homeland defense among the states and the federal government. It seemed the perfect venue for bringing attention to the illegal immigration crisis in Arizona. And, as luck would have it, the council was having its first meeting in Washington on June 2, 2010.

As I prepared to go to Washington, I again reached out to the White House for a meeting. But a White House spokesperson said the president's schedule wouldn't "allow for a meeting" with me and my team, although in true Washington, D.C., fashion, he did leave the door open to "sit down with the governor in the future." That same week, I noticed, the president's schedule included a fund-raising event in Pittsburgh, a reception for Major League Soccer, and a concert at the White House to honor Paul McCartney. *I know he's the cute Beatle and all*, I thought, *but we're in serious trouble here!* (That was the same concert, by the way, in which McCartney said that George W. Bush didn't know "what a library is." The audience applauded, and Obama grinned.)

Before I left Phoenix, I sat down for an interview with a young reporter from the *Arizona Republic*. As we talked about SB 1070 and all of the unending attacks, especially the "Nazi" name calling, I spoke about how much they hurt in light of my father's service during World War II and his subsequent death. This is what the *Arizona Republic* reported: "'The Nazi comments . . . they are awful,' she said, her voice dropping. 'Knowing that my father died fighting the Nazi regime in Germany, that I lost him when I was 11 because of that . . . and then to have them call me Hitler's daughter. It hurts. It's ugliness beyond anything I've ever experienced.'"

It was the statement that my father had died "fighting the Nazi regime" that set off the firestorm. It sounded as if I was saying that my father had died in Germany, not after having served as a civilian here at home. That wasn't my intention, and I believe the reporter simply misunderstood what I had said. But a single statement can make a world of difference when the media is looking for an excuse to pounce. This was their excuse.

This reporter was new to the job and had never heard my life story. She had an excuse. Others who took advantage of the statement . . . not so much. Arizona Democratic Party spokeswoman Jennifer Johnson smelled blood and attacked. "It seems obvious that Jan Brewer stretched the truth to make herself a more sympathetic figure." The liberal media began sliming me as a liar. *Vanity Fair* snarked, "The saga is very sad, except its tragedy is somewhat mitigated by the fact that it is extremely untrue." *Newsweek* lumped me in with Connecticut Senate candidate Richard Blumenthal, who lied outright about his military service, and Illinois Senate candidate Mark Kirk, who served in Iraq but said during his campaign that he had been fired upon while doing so.

As I listened to the media trying to sully my father's memory, I struggled to keep my anger at bay. My dad wasn't a superhero; he didn't have a Medal of Honor. But he was my hero. I lived on a military base; I saw soldiers being deployed, and some of them never came back. The last thing I would ever do is try to cheapen *their* memory. Finally, I released a statement trying to put the matter to rest. "Even in the end, when my dad struggled for breath, he never regretted serving his country, helping free Europe from Hitler's grip," I wrote. "I have proudly recounted his story in many places for many years. My father's patriotism and sacrifice need no embellishment."

That night, I flew to D.C. When I hit the ground, I found out that President Obama had agreed to meet with me.

The people of Arizona were finally going to get their fifteen minutes with the leader of the free world.

According to the White House, an unexpected opening had occurred in the president's schedule. If you ask me, the president had bowed under pressure. But whatever the reason, I was excited by the opportunity to explain the impact that illegal immigration was having on Arizona and the rest of America. That night on CNN, John King asked what my number-one request would be of the president. You won't be shocked at my answer.

"Mr. President, we need our borders secured."

The next day, I tried for the most part to keep out of the public eye. I attended the Council of Governors meeting, where the topics of discussion were kept largely secret. That night, though, I appeared again on Greta Van Susteren's Fox show to preview the meeting with President Obama. Greta asked a question that struck a chord with me: Was this just a photo op? "How do you tomorrow make sure that you're not being used?" Greta asked.

It was a good question. I told her I just had to trust that the president was sincere about wanting to hear from me. In any case, it was an opportunity I couldn't pass up. "I think it's important to not only the state of Arizona but to all of America that we are able to tell him exactly what is taking place down there in Arizona and that we need to have our borders secured," I said. Greta said that she thought Obama had been cornered. I told her, honestly, that I would take the meeting any way I could get it.

"You don't seem very afraid," Greta noted. "Are you going to be in awe when you walk into that Oval Office, or are you going to be just as tough tomorrow with the president?"

I explained that I had been in the White House when Ronald Reagan was president and during the presidencies of both Bushes. Then I used a saying that is familiar to everyone who knows me. "It's not my first rodeo with the president of the United States."

That night at our hotel, we got the list of people who would be at the meeting. White House senior adviser Valerie Jarrett would be there. So would the president's chief of staff, Pete Rouse, and the director of the National Counterterrorism Center, John Brennan. I also noticed another name on the list: White House counsel Bob Bauer. I was puzzled, because I had been told that there wouldn't be any discussion of the lawsuit they were hinting at filing against us. I had good, trusted aides with me: my deputy director of communications, Kim Sabow, and my deputy chief of staff for operations, Brian McNeil. But still, if they were going to have their lawyer, I was going to have my lawyer. So I had my general counsel, Joe Kanefield, get on a red-eye from Phoenix.

At the hotel that night, everyone was trying to prep me, to grill me, to get me ready. It filled the air with tension. At a certain point I said, "You know what? I'm through. I'm going to bed." I knew what I was going to say, and my staff was getting me—and themselves—all wound up. There's nothing like leaving things in the hands of God and getting a good night's rest.

Joe arrived the next morning, bleary-eyed from lack of sleep. Still, his lawyerly instincts were sharp. Despite what we had heard, Joe anticipated that they would bring up the lawsuit. He

planned to tell them that there had already been multiple lawsuits filed against the state by civil rights groups and others, and
it made little sense for the U.S. government to weigh in. We also
weren't sure that the White House staff understood my executive order and the language in the bill that was meant to ensure
that it wasn't a license to profile. We planned to encourage them
to let the law go into effect and see that the protections we had
built into it would work. If they didn't, they could challenge the
law as applied. "President Obama is a lawyer and former constitutional law professor, right?" I said. "So he's got to get it."

As we drove up to the White House, I groaned at what I saw.
Our old friends in the Service Employees International Union
had set up a protest outside. They were chanting, "Governor Jan
Brewer, shame on you!" And, of course, "Yes, we can!" These
were President Obama's biggest supporters. The head of the
SEIU, Andy Stern, had visited the White House more than any
other person during the first six months of the president's term.
The union's opposition to SB 1070 was no secret—their finger-
prints were all over the Astroturf protests and boycotts. Still, I
was astounded that they had followed me all the way to Washington. What were they so afraid of? Their stance against SB
1070 didn't make any sense—after all, the people most hurt by
illegal immigration are union workers, whose job prospects are
undercut by businesses that hire illegals in order to avoid paying
minimum wage. But the SEIU and its allies are liberals, first and
foremost, and their chief goal is the legalization of millions of
potential Democratic voters and union members.

When we got to the White House, we were sent into a holding
room outside the Oval Office. One of my staffers took pictures.
That was apparently a no-no. The Secret Service confiscated all

of our cell phones and cameras. Too bad we weren't illegal aliens, or we could have sued them. As we waited, we chatted with a Marine guard who, it turned out, was from Arizona. He told us he was very proud to see his governor in the White House. I was flattered and encouraged. It was a good sign, I thought.

An aide came in and told us the president would see us now. We walked around a short curve in the hallway . . . and there was the president, standing outside his office to greet us. Inside, seated in a line in front of his desk, were Jarrett, Brennan, Rouse, and Bauer.

We sat down and started with some chitchat. But after a few minutes the president's tone got serious—and condescending. He proceeded to lecture me about everything he was doing to promote "comprehensive immigration reform," which was code for encouraging more illegal immigration by letting those already in the country illegally jump the line. He said they were doing everything they could, but the system was broken. He didn't mention the violence on the border, the drug cartels, or the enormous costs being borne by the citizens of states like Arizona. He mentioned that the Department of Justice was reviewing SB 1070 and that he was leaving to them the decision whether to sue. "I will not put my finger on the scales of justice with regard to this review," he said. "I have completely delegated the decision to them." Joe and I exchanged a glance. We were skeptical, to say the least.

It wasn't long before I realized I was hearing the president's stump speech. Only I was supposed to listen without talking. Did he care to hear the view from the actual scene at the border? Did the opinions and observations of the people of Arizona mean anything to him? I didn't think so. His mind seemed made up.

If he knew about the escalating levels of violence, the kidnappings, the drop houses, the home invasions, the spotters, and the drug mules, he didn't give any indication. It was as though President Obama thought he would lecture me and I would learn at his knee. He was patronizing. He understood that we were "frustrated," he said—heck, yes, we were frustrated!—but he didn't seem interested in knowing why. Then it dawned on me: *He's treating me like the cop he had over for a beer after he bad-mouthed the Cambridge police*, I thought. *He thinks he can humor me and then get rid of me.*

I listened to about ten minutes of this. Finally the president's lecture ended and it was my turn. I hadn't interrupted the president because I respect the office, and I was determined to show respect. But now I was ready to give him a piece of my mind.

"I have written five letters to your administration, and I haven't received one reply," I told him. He seemed genuinely shocked about that, and said he didn't know. He assured me it wouldn't happen again. I found out later that within minutes of our meeting, the government affairs office at the White House had called my office requesting copies of our letters. Better late than never!

I pointed out that the law he had called "misguided" was a mirror of the federal law against illegal immigration. I told him that the people of Arizona supported what we were trying to do, as did a majority of the American people. I didn't want to talk about "comprehensive immigration reform" while our border was out of control, I said. After we had secured the border, then we could discuss what comes next. If he saw it differently, we would just have to disagree.

Before we left, I asked the president to come to Arizona and see the border for himself. I still believed that he would view the issue differently if he could just see it with his own eyes. "It's very different from what you see on TV or read in the paper," I said. President Obama wouldn't commit to a visit, but he did promise to get back to me with some further ideas. Considering that I had never received a response from his administration before, I considered that progress.

Despite the president's lecturing tone and lack of commitment, I left the meeting feeling elated. If nothing else, the people of Arizona had finally been heard. I was eager to speak to the press gathered outside. "Governor, there's a lot of press out there," Kim Sabow said to me as we left the White House. "What do you mean by 'a lot'?" I asked. "I mean *a lot*," she said. "They need more time to make room for everyone."

When I finally stepped outside, there was more media gathered than I had ever addressed before. I knew that what I said would be important, not just for Arizona but for the whole country, in determining how we dealt with this issue going forward.

"We agreed to try to work together in order to find some solutions," I said. "We know that we're not going to agree on certain issues until other issues are worked out. And so we're going to begin some more direct dialogue in a couple of weeks."

I decided to swallow my misgivings and give the president the benefit of the doubt. "I am encouraged that there is going to be much better dialogue between the federal government and the state of Arizona," I repeated. "I hope that's not wishful thinking. I hope that's positive thinking." I was asked whether I thought Obama had read the law. I smiled and took the next question.

We went back to Arizona allowing ourselves to feel victorious. We had forced the president of the United States to

hear the voices of people who were being victimized by illegal immigration. We eagerly awaited his ideas for securing
the border.

It may be politics as usual that governors of the opposing
party don't get treated the same way as those from the governing
party. Maybe in Washington it's just normal to say one thing and
do another. But that's not the way we do business in Arizona.
And so we waited, patiently, for the response from the Obama
White House that we had been promised.

Two weeks later, we got our response—but it wasn't exactly
what we had expected. It came in the form of signs posted by
federal bureaucrats on Arizona lands a full eighty miles in from
the border. Here's what the signs said:

DANGER—PUBLIC WARNING
TRAVEL NOT RECOMMENDED

- *Active Drug and Human Smuggling Area*
- *Visitors May Encounter Armed Criminals and
Smuggling Vehicles Traveling at High Rates of Speed*
- *Stay Away from Trash, Clothing, Backpacks, and
Abandoned Vehicles*
- *If You See Suspicious Activity, DO NOT
CONFRONT! Move Away and Call 911*
- *BLM Encourages Visitors to Use Public Lands North of
Interstate 8*
- *For More Information, call 623-580-5500*

The president had promised fresh ideas. What we'd gotten
instead were warnings to the American people from their own
government telling them not to venture onto their own land. We

wanted help in defending our border, and instead we got the white flag of surrender.

Against the advice of my security detail, I traveled to an area where one of these signs had been posted, about eighty miles from the border, just off I-8. While there, I spoke directly to the president in a video posted on YouTube.

"What is our country coming to?" I asked. "We will not surrender any part of Arizona. We need to stand up and demand action. Washington is broken, Mr. President. Do your job. Secure our borders. Arizona and the nation are waiting."

CHAPTER FIVE

Sued for Enforcing the Law

I learned on television from Ecuador that I was being sued by the federal government.

That's right—*television from Ecuador.* On June 8, just a few days after my meeting with President Obama, Secretary of State Hillary Clinton was in Ecuador being interviewed. The first question, right out of the box, was about SB 1070. Here's how she responded: "President Obama has spoken out against the law because he thinks that the federal government should be determining immigration policy. And the Justice Department, under his direction, will be bringing a lawsuit against the act."

It was unbelievable. I had just been told by President Obama that the decision whether or not to sue us was under review at the DOJ and he would not attempt to influence the outcome. Yet now Secretary Clinton was boasting that it had been the president's own decision. And not only wouldn't the president tell me to my face, the White House didn't even have the decency to let me know before I heard it on national television. (Later, the choice of Ecuador to announce the lawsuit made more sense. When the administration had reported SB 1070 to the United Nations Human Rights Council, Ecuador was the first country that charged racial profiling; and when the Ecuadorans set up a consulate in Arizona, they made clear that they were doing so to aid illegal aliens—to help their citizens break our law.)

The Obama administration was behaving as if its duty to another country was greater than its duty to the residents of Arizona. "This is no way to treat the people of Arizona," I said after I heard about the lawsuit. "To learn of this lawsuit through an Ecuadoran interview with the secretary of state is just outrageous. If our own government intends to sue our state to prevent illegal immigration enforcement, the least it can do is inform us before it informs the citizens of another nation."

I was outraged by the administration's high-handed treatment, but I wasn't actually surprised about the lawsuit. They'd been hinting about it for months. Six lawsuits by groups including the ACLU had already been filed against SB 1070. These suits covered just about every conceivable legal angle, but we were pretty sure the administration would add theirs to the list. They had been . . . to put it nicely . . . *misrepresenting* SB 1070 for months. They had all but called us racists for passing it. Why wouldn't they sue to prevent its being implemented?

The question of how the state of Arizona would defend itself against these suits was one of the more surreal parts of this saga. Our elected attorney general—my attorney general—was a Democrat named Terry Goddard who from day one had made no secret of his hostility toward SB 1070. Goddard would normally be the official responsible for defending the state against a lawsuit. The problem was that he had already declared the law "unconstitutional" and said that he would have vetoed it. And to top it off, he announced in January that he was running for governor on the Democratic ticket. That's what I mean by surreal. Here I was, facing a federal lawsuit over the most controversial state law in the country, the state's attorney general refused to defend us, and he was trying to take my job.

Terry and I had been down this road before. A few months earlier, when Arizona joined the lawsuit against the president's sweeping health care law, Terry had refused to join the challenge. I had to go to the legislature to get the authority to speak for the state in that lawsuit. Now the same thing was happening, but this time with a law duly passed by his own legislature and supported by 70 percent of his fellow Arizonans.

Still, Goddard ridiculously insisted that he could defend the state against any challenge to the law. I insisted he could not. Having him in charge, I argued, would be like a lawyer saying that his client was guilty of murder but that he would defend him anyway. It didn't make sense for me or for the state of Arizona, and I wasn't going to have it.

The last straw was when a team from the Justice Department came out to Phoenix, supposedly to brief us on how their "review" of the law was going. They had requested the meeting, and my legal counsel, Joe Kanefield, prepared to meet with them. It was an opportunity to try to talk them out of filing a lawsuit. But just before the meeting, Joe turned on the radio to hear Terry Goddard holding a press conference describing *his* meeting with the team from the DOJ. He had gone behind our backs and had a secret meeting with the very people who were threatening to sue us. That was it. We promptly issued a press release questioning the "curious coordination" between the Democratic candidate for governor and the Obama Justice Department. I called on Terry to recuse himself from the case. He eventually relented and removed himself from the case, but only after he had tied himself in rhetorical knots trying to argue that he was right on both counts: The law *was* unconstitutional, but he should still be the one to defend it in court.

•   •   •

On July 6, 2010, the Obama administration formally filed its lawsuit. It named me alongside the State of Arizona as a defendant. I didn't realize the enormity of it until the first day in court, when I heard the bailiff say the words "the United States of America versus the State of Arizona and Janice K. Brewer." My country versus me! How did this happen?

In my own view, America was the true defendant. This wasn't *U.S. v. Arizona and Janice K. Brewer*; this was the Obama administration against the pro-U.S. state of Arizona. It would be absolutely incoherent to suggest that the United States was standing against itself—which is what the name of the case suggested. How could the United States stand against its own borders? How could it stand against its own values? It couldn't.

Simply put, the case was misnamed. It was *Obama v. the People of the United States*. Fully half of Americans opposed the DOJ's lawsuit, with only 33 percent supporting it. And 61 percent liked the idea of their own state passing a law similar to SB 1070.

I made a point of being in court for the hearings. I sat in the front row, right behind the counsel I'd hired to represent the state. I wasn't going to let Terry Goddard try to defend a law he thought was unconstitutional, but I also didn't want the taxpayers of Arizona to have to pick up the cost of another lawyer. So I set up a legal defense fund—KeepAZSafe.com—to raise money to pay for our lawyer. Supporters were already sending us money, and I thought this would be a good use for it. Every time I went on Greta Van Susteren's show and mentioned the fund, contributions would pour in the next day. They came from all over the country. It was very, very encouraging to see the support we had.

The press tried to make an issue out of the fact that I personally attended the court hearings. They said it was grandstanding. But I replied that I needed to be there to represent the people of Arizona, who overwhelmingly supported the law. Also, I said, the Obama administration had gone out if its way to name me as a defendant, and defendants have the right to confront their accusers. That seemed to quiet them down.

I had a front-row seat for the Obama administration's case against SB 1070, and from a legal perspective it was absolutely absurd. The lawsuit is what's known as a "peremptory challenge," meaning that the administration was contending that the law was invalid before it had a chance to go into effect. We had hoped that they would wait to see whether all the careful protections against racial profiling that we had built into the law and the executive order accompanying it would work. That was what they had said they were concerned about: racial profiling. We had taken their concerns seriously and carefully crafted a law that explicitly prohibited profiling. Why not seek to redress any issues at the enforcement stage? That was how the federal oversight process was supposed to function, instead of abrogating the duly enacted will of the people of Arizona.

I know now that the Obama administration was never interested in seeing whether SB 1070 could actually work as designed. Heck, maybe they were afraid it would work too well. I think they wanted to send a message to all the other states that were thinking about passing a similar law—as well as to Hispanic voters in other states, and to the world at large. After all, if enough states started enforcing federal immigration law, eventually the law would actually mean something, and I don't think they ever wanted that.

The surprising thing was, after all the talk about racial pro-filing, when the Obama administration finally filed its lawsuit, it was based on completely different grounds. After raging for months about civil rights and discrimination against Hispanic families going out for ice cream, when push came to shove, they made the fairly technical argument that our state law was un-constitutional because it was preempted by federal law. They cited the supremacy clause of the Constitution, which states that federal laws made under the Constitution "shall be the supreme law of the land" and that states cannot trump federal law. This makes sense: We wouldn't want states to be able to simply over-ride every law made by the federal government. Otherwise it would have no power at all. As Alexander Hamilton said in the Federalist Papers, the supremacy clause "only declares a truth, which flows immediately and necessarily from the institution of a federal government."

So how could the government use this clause to argue that our state law, which essentially *enforced* federal law—and whose language was taken directly from the federal statute—was un-constitutional? They were forced to argue that the federal gov-ernment and the state of Arizona had different ideas regarding what enforcement means. Which is to say, they made the reveal-ing argument that SB 1070 enforced the law *too much*.

The DOJ singled out one provision of the law to make this case. SB 1070 allows Arizonans to collect money damages—to sue—by showing that any state official or agency has adopted a policy that "limits or restricts the enforcement of federal immi-gration laws . . . to less than the full extent permitted by federal law." On the face of it, this provision is designed to push "en-forcement of federal immigration laws." So what's the problem?

By enforcing federal immigration law, the feds argued, we were pursuing "only one goal—'attrition'—and ignor[ing] the many other objectives that Congress has established for the federal immigration law." But what other objectives are there to our illegal immigration law besides preventing and punishing illegal immigration? It was an insane argument.

What the Obama administration was arguing was that Arizona's enforcement of federal immigration law *violated* federal immigration law because the federal government had chosen *not to enforce* federal immigration law. Got it? In other words, Congress can pass a law, and the enforcement arm of the executive branch can decide not to do anything about it. Moreover, they argued that their decision *not* to enforce the law has the same legal authority as what was actually passed in writing. In effect, then, by passing federal laws, the feds can prevent states from passing their own laws on the same issue. Then, by not enforcing the very federal laws they've passed, the feds can prevent the states from enforcing the federal laws.

For example, let's say that the federal government decided to pass a law preventing people from growing marijuana. Then they decided they didn't really care about marijuana, so they weren't going to do anything to enforce the law. Your state then decides to do the job the feds won't, and sends police officers to raid a local pot farm. The federal government can now argue that the state was violating federal law by *enforcing* federal law.

The feds didn't stop with this insane argument. They also fell back into the "racial profiling" nonsense we'd debunked time and again. But to do that, they had to engage in a series of ridiculous hypotheticals. They claimed that the law would "cause the detention and harassment of authorized visitors, immigrants, and citizens who do not have or carry identification documents." Really? Federal law already requires that immigrants carry proof of their legal status. And as for legal residents and citizens, when was the last time you got stopped by a police officer without your license or ID and *weren't* harassed or detained?

They also said the law would "interfere with vital foreign policy and national security interests by disrupting the United States' relationship with Mexico and other countries." On this one, they were sort of telling the truth, seeing as how Mexico doesn't want to do anything to shut the border. In fact, the feds cited President Calderón's demagogic speech before Congress as evidence that SB 1070 "subjected the United States to direct criticism by other countries and international organizations." So criticism from other countries suddenly qualifies as a reason to strike down a law, according to the Department of Justice. The impact on foreign policy of a state law is utterly irrelevant to its legality under the Constitution. Many domestic laws have an impact on international relations; that doesn't mean they're all unconstitutional.

The foolishness continued as the lawsuit went on. The Department of Justice claimed that the Obama administration understood our concerns and had "undertaken significant efforts to secure our nation's borders"—nice-sounding words from an administration that had repeatedly ignored our pleas for aid and was now seeking to punish us for taking matters into our own hands. They further claimed that by asking for ID after a legal stop for another offense, we'd be placing burdens on immigrants who might be in the country legally but without papers because they hadn't received them yet. This hypothetical case was so weak that the government itself had called a similar argument in a different case "patently absurd," saying that it would result in "wholly emasculated law enforcement." They also argued that we were regulating immigration, when in fact we were regulating law enforcement's approach to illegal aliens—meaning that we were concerned only with people who were already in violation of a criminal offense. SB 1070 doesn't deal with who should remain in the United States or who is here legally—that's the feds' job.

What most revealed the desperation of the Obama administration's case was what its lawsuit *didn't* argue—namely, that the law violated the Fourteenth Amendment, the part of the Constitution that ensures the equal protection of the law. The Fourteenth Amendment is often invoked in civil rights cases, because such cases normally charge that certain individuals aren't being treated equally under the law. Obama, Holder, and Napolitano had all specifically complained that the law was inevitably going to violate some people's civil rights—that it was going to discriminate based on race or ethnicity—but in the end they didn't invoke the one clause of the Constitution that is most often cited in such cases. Weird, right?

Not really. They knew there was no civil rights violation here, especially since I had signed an executive order that specifically dealt with implementing SB 1070 in a nondiscriminatory manner. Instead, they based their entire case on the claim that the law was unconstitutional because it was preempted by federal authority.

The truth is that the Arizona law is deeply rooted in constitutional principles. The Constitution gives Congress the power to "establish a uniform Rule of Naturalization," which can be interpreted to encompass the power to control the borders.

Furthermore, the whole purpose of the federal government is to "provide for the common defense" and to "insure domestic tranquility," which in turn requires the feds to ensure the safety of citizens with regard to border issues. Even more to the point, as I've mentioned, Article IV, Section 4, says that the federal government "shall protect each of [the states] against Invasion." That's what we in Arizona are undergoing—an invasion across our borders.

Let me be clear (as the president likes to say): The federal government has the obligation to secure our border. But if the feds decide to act as if they don't, the states don't have to lie down and take the consequences. According to the Tenth Amendment, "The powers not delegated to the United States by the Constitution, nor prohibited by it to the States, are reserved to the States respectively, or to the people." Now, if the feds want to argue that they don't have that obligation under the Constitution, then under the Tenth Amendment, Arizona obviously should take control of its own destiny. We have a duty to our citizens, and if the feds choose to abdicate theirs, we are not obliged to do the same. Yet that was precisely what the Obama administration was arguing: They didn't have to take responsibility for the border, but we couldn't, either. In the end, what was really at issue in the government's case was simply the assertion of their monopoly of power—a power it defined as essentially arbitrary.

There was one line in the lawsuit that I thought summed up the administration's case more clearly than any other. The Arizona law, it said, "conflict[s] with and undermines the federal government's careful balance of immigration enforcement priorities and objectives." Our "priorities and objectives" in passing SB 1070 were to enforce the law and have another tool to secure the border. The

Obama administration was not only admitting that it had different priorities. It was asserting that the federal government knows best, that its assessment of priorities is based on superior judgment, and that the states just have to live with the results.

I couldn't help but be reminded that the same arrogant bureaucratic mentality had created this problem in the first place, when anonymous federal bureaucrats decided to funnel the stream of illegal immigration toward the Arizona border. They had done this without consulting us, made no provision for our safety and security, and ignored our repeated requests for assistance, and now they had declared war on us by way of the press and the courts for trying to deal with the problem ourselves. Behold your federal government at work!

As I read the government's lawsuit, it came to me that this fight isn't about "preemption," federalism, or even civil rights. It is about what kind of country we're going to have.

When he wasn't warning about the dangers of racial profiling, President Obama has consistently argued that laws like SB 1070 would create a "patchwork" of state immigration laws that would bring chaos to the system—as if the system could get more chaotic. I've always found it interesting that SB 1070, which merely enforces existing federal law, creates a dreaded "patchwork," while the laws passed by cities such as New York, Chicago, and San Francisco to declare themselves "sanctuary cities"—where police are explicitly barred from inquiring about immigration status and enforcing the law—haven't raised a peep of protest. The message being sent is very clear: "Patchworks" are bad when state and local laws merely reinforce the federal law; but when they purposefully subvert the federal law, they're no problem at all.

I've thought for a long time about the reason behind this double standard. A lot has been written and said about how President Obama's treatment of immigration—and plenty of other officials' as well—is purely political, that it's just aimed at the next election. And there's no denying that the administration's lawsuit came along at a time when the president's approval ratings among Hispanics were falling, after he'd failed in his promise to address immigration reform during his first year in office. But I think we let the president and his liberal allies off too easily when we ascribe their motivation to mere politics. There is a point at which politics becomes policy, and policy determines the kind of country we have.

What I mean to say is that the cynical politics of immigration has real-world consequences for our country—*intended* consequences. Eventually, the government's failure to secure the border becomes a policy of purposefully *not* securing the border, a policy of actively encouraging illegal aliens. That's where I think our government is today.

Take the unions, which have been the main organizational and financial force behind the fight against SB 1070. They were the ones Astroturfing the protests and sending buses to my house and protestors to the White House for my visit with President Obama. On the face of it, of course, their concern with protecting illegal immigration doesn't make sense. Union workers have some of the best-paid jobs in the United States, with great benefits, and they're the first people whose position gets undermined when businesses hire illegal aliens to do the work Americans supposedly "won't do." Samuel Gompers, who founded the

American Federation of Labor, saw that back in 1924 when he wrote, "Every effort to enact immigration [reform] must expect to meet a number of hostile forces and, in particular ... corporation employers who desire to employ physical strength ... at the lowest wage and who prefer a rapidly revolving labor supply at low wages to a regular supply of American wage earners at fair wages."

Gompers was talking about an influx of legal immigrants, not illegal immigrants. But for unions, the logic is even stronger for those who break the law to get here. Unions can survive in a free market only when there is no cheap supply of labor undercutting them. In 1981, the AFL-CIO recognized this, stating, "Illegal workers take jobs away from American workers and they undermine U.S. wages and working conditions." Why would they stand up for a policy that makes it easier for them to be undercut?

The first reason is simple opportunism. Whereas the unions used to have more conservative members (they were once known as Reagan Democrats), today their membership is different. So the union bosses have made the strategic decision to make themselves the organizational arm of the Democratic Party. The SEIU and their allies are political buddies with the people in the Obama administration, and they want to make sure that their friends keep getting elected so they can throw them more rich union contracts.

Just look at SEIU vice president Eliseo Medina. On April 25, 2010, he showed up at a protest rally at the Arizona Capitol to denounce SB 1070 as "an unjust law." He did a rabble-rousing routine in front of a cheering crowd. "There is no place for discrimination, for hate and intolerance in America!" he yelled.

The enemy, he assured the crowd, wasn't just me; it was all Republicans. "Governor Brewer and the Republican Party have declared war on Latinos and on immigrants! They don't care about human and civil rights," he screamed.

Then he got to his point, which was, of course, that nobody who cares about civil rights, the poor, or puppies and kittens should ever vote Republican. "Governor Brewer and the Republican Party, you have voted against us! It's our turn now!" he bellowed. "In the next couple of days, they are going to know that we are not defenseless. There cannot be one single Latino vote for any Republican, whether for U.S. Senate, governor, legislature, or dog catcher!"

Medina's partisan turn at the SB 1070 rally was just his latest attempt to gin up votes for his Democratic paymasters. His speech reminded me of one that he had made in June 2009 at an event for the Campaign for America's Future, a union-allied liberal advocacy group. It was here that he laid out, in stark black and white, the reason for the unions' passionate support of continued illegal immigration: more Democratic voters.

"[When] we reform the immigration laws, it puts twelve million people on the path to citizenship and eventually voters," he said. Medina also reminded the crowd (which needed no reminding) that Latinos and immigrants had overwhelmingly supported "progressive" candidates in 2008. Barack Obama got two out of every three of their votes.

"Can you imagine if we have the same turnout and we have eight million new voters who care about our issues and will be voting?" Medina said, practically salivating over the prospect of creating "a governing coalition for the long term, not just for an election cycle." Leaving the border open, he said with startling candor, would "solidify and expand the progressive coalition for the future."

An SEIU Local 1877 sign spotted at a recent Los Angeles rally in favor of amnesty for illegal immigration sums up this strategy nicely: TODAY WE MARCH, TOMORROW WE VOTE!

Democratic interest group politics lead to an open-border policy, which leads in turn to a different America.

Somebody's thinking beyond the next election.

There's yet another reason for the unions' seemingly contradictory support of illegal immigration. Unions—particularly public employee unions—support it because it serves their interests to have a permanent class of people who are financially dependent on the government.

The sad secret about private sector unions is that they are dying. There used to be a reason for private sector unions—like, for instance, protecting people like my dad from inhaling the toxic materials at the munitions plant, which eventually killed him. But in today's world, such unions have become basically obsolete. All they do now is drive up the cost of doing business, thereby preventing their own members from getting hired. Arizona is what we call a "right to work" state. As mandated by the Arizona Constitution, Arizonans are free to join a union or not—it's their choice, not some union boss's command. And interestingly enough, when employees are given the choice of whether or not to join a union, they increasingly say no. These workers understand that the rigid workplace rules and regulations that unions promote are bad for growth, bad for competitiveness, and bad for jobs.

More and more workers recognize this. That's why in the private sector, where employees have a real stake in the success of the businesses they work for, only 7.5 percent of workers are unionized. By contrast, more than 36 percent of public sector workers are unionized, and more than 42 percent of local government workers. That's because public sector workers in the federal government don't have to worry about unemployment. Ever. In many federal agencies, the primary threat to job security is actually death. The job security for all federal workers in 2010 was 99.43 percent. It's even higher for workers who have been on the job for more than a few years. With the government this bloated, the best guarantee of never-ending employment is a government paycheck. The average government worker has a tenure nearly twice as long as that of the average private sector worker.

Democratic Party bosses love government workers because each of those workers must rely upon the health and growth of government to pay his salary and guarantee his benefits. If the government contracts or shuts down for any reason, those workers are out of a job. And public sector unions love the Democratic bosses because they keep on growing government. The more people the Democrats can put on the payroll, the more voters they can lock up for their candidates.

That gives public sector unions like the SEIU (which includes huge numbers of public employees) unbelievable leverage. Because the party bosses want to keep government workers employed and happy, they'll give the unions just about anything they want. And the best part (for them) is that it doesn't cost them a thing. The taxpayers pick up the tab. Liberal politicians spend taxpayer money to grow government; the unions keep voting for (and contributing to) Democrats, and the Democrats stay in office so they can spend more of the taxpayers' money growing government. It's a simple, corrupt, mutual back-scratching circle.

How does illegal immigration play into this? Most illegal aliens work hard. That is not in dispute. But the unfortunate fact is that most illegal aliens are also unskilled and uneducated. Unskilled workers have higher unemployment rates and lower earnings. Many rely on government programs to help support them and their families. Either that or they rely on government jobs—if they can get them. In either case, they are more dependent on government than either legal immigrants or the native-born. Households headed by illegal aliens collect more welfare, due to their generally lower education levels and incomes compared with native-born households. Much of this access to the welfare system by these households is gained through their American-born children, who are U.S. citizens. That means more government, which means more public sector union members.

Even if, in the short term, more illegal immigration means fewer union jobs, the unions are okay with that. It is a strategic cost they are willing to bear. Because they know that if the Democrats keep winning, they will give the unions subsidies, grow government, and employ more union members.

Some of the unions', especially the SEIU's, massive opposition to SB 1070 may have a more personal motivation. As we waited around for Janet Napolitano to resign and leave, she gave a parting gift to the public employee unions. She issued her final executive order granting something called "meet and confer" status to many of the public employee unions. That mandates that the union's chosen representatives meet at least once a quarter with state agency heads. I repealed the executive order as soon as I became governor, citing its potential impact on trimming our bloated budget and its conflict with our state's right-to-work guarantee.

Whatever their motivation, it is unforgivable for public sector unions and the Democratic Party to use illegal aliens as a way to ensure their power base. But use them they do. In the condescending belief that illegal aliens will become prompt and permanent clients of big government, thus adding to their power, unions spend their members' dues (which in the case of public sector unions are provided by the taxpayers) overwhelmingly on Democrats. Unions are by far the biggest contributors to political candidates and parties. In the twenty years between 1989 and 2009, the unions gave almost $500 million in political contributions, and about $450 million of that was to Democrats. It will surprise most mainstream-media-consuming Americans to know that the unions' closest competition for political influence, the financial investment industry, gave less than half of what labor contributed between 1989 and 2009. Unions are the country's biggest political investors, and they have invested big in the Democratic Party.

This investment has been handsomely rewarded. It's why Democrats kill free-trade bills. It's why they push "stimulus" bills for less than "shovel-ready" jobs. It's why they support the program known as card check, a kneecapping method designed to allow union intimidation of anti-union workers. And the union's support of Democrats is why it came as no surprise to us that when Arizona voters overwhelmingly approved an amendment to our state constitution to require unions to allow members to vote by secret ballot, the Obama administration filed yet another lawsuit against Arizona to stop it.

President Obama has forced the auto companies to hand over the keys to the United Auto Workers instead of to the creditors who were first in line. The administration has used the National Labor Relations Board in an attempt to shut down a Boeing plant located in South Carolina because South Carolina is a right-to-work state.

And when it comes to immigration, President Obama has made no secret about where he gets his marching orders. As a candidate, Obama spoke to the SEIU and announced, "Your agenda has been my agenda in the United States Senate. Before debating health care, I talked to Andy Stern and SEIU members. Before immigration debates took place in Washington, I talked with Eliseo Medina and SEIU members." This was a frank admission that the Obama administration would be run by the SEIU. It wasn't a tacit deal. It was open and clear-cut. *Support me and I'll do your bidding in Washington.* And when you think about it, it's a win-win proposition. Open borders and amnesty for illegal aliens create more voters for President Obama and more members for the SEIU. This larger power base allows them both to pursue their shared agenda: bigger, more expansive government. That may be a win-win for the president and the unions, but it's a big loser for the American taxpayers. It's also dishonest. If President Obama and his allies really wanted to have an honest debate about illegal immigration, they would say openly that they believe our country's future should be determined by an uncontrolled, illegal influx of immigrants. But they won't say that. Instead they pretend to care about border security while working to actively undermine it. It's dishonest, dangerous, and undemocratic. America's fate should be in the hands of Americans, not human smugglers and drug cartels.

Beyond being a home to bigger and more expensive government, the America being created by advocates of illegal immigration (or of failing to prevent it, which amounts to the same thing) is one defined more by ethnic and tribal differences than by the common values that have always united Americans. In Arizona, we've seen this evolution up close in our battle to keep the teaching of race hatred out of our public schools.

In the second half of the 1990s, the Tucson Unified School District quietly adopted something called La Raza Studies. "La Raza" means "race" in Spanish, and as the name implies, La Raza Studies is part of the larger commitment to multiculturalism that is popular among liberals and many professional educators.

"Multiculturalism" sounds like a nice, friendly word that means respect for others. In practice, however, it's worked out very differently. Multiculturalism encourages its followers to put racial and ethnic identity above all. It says that assimilation into American values is wrong and misguided—even racist. It says that requiring everyone to abide by our laws is xenophobic. Multiculturalism and the open-borders philosophy go hand in hand. As President Obama said to President Calderón, "In the twenty-first century, we are defined not by our borders but by our bonds." This is just wrong. We are defined by our values, which define both our borders and our bonds. And as the poet Robert Frost once wrote, "Good fences make good neighbors."

Advocates of the La Raza Studies curriculum claim that it is just a way to teach largely Hispanic public school children their own history. But when my current attorney general, Tom Horne, was Arizona superintendent of public instruction in 2007, he found something very different going on in the program. Tucson school officials at first resisted allowing Tom to see the textbooks they use in the La Raza Studies curriculum. When they finally relented, he found a curriculum of grievance and distortion that was being taught in Tucson public schools under the guise of history.

According to Horne, the students were being taught "that Arizona and other states were stolen from Mexico and should be given back." One of the textbooks Tom finally pried from the hands of the Tucson school district was Rodolfo Acuña's *Occupied America*, a title that conveys the notion that Anglo Americans are illegitimate occupiers. Another textbook was titled *Pedagogy of the Oppressed*, by a famous anticolonialist writer named Paolo Freire. One former Tucson history teacher, John Ward, reported that the focus of La Raza Studies was to teach students that "Mexican-Americans were and continue to be victims of a racist American society driven by the interests of middle and upper-class whites." One student who took the classes put it memorably: "I didn't realize I was oppressed. Now that I took this class, I realize that I am oppressed."

"By the time I left that class, I saw a change [in the students]," Ward said. "An angry tone. They taught them not to trust their teachers, not to trust the system. They taught them the system wasn't worth trusting."

Tom, who had marched on Washington with Martin Luther King Jr. as a teenager in 1963, was deeply disturbed by this violation of King's call to judge people by the content of their character rather than the color of their skin. In the name of multicultural tolerance, the La Raza Studies classes were teaching students racial intolerance. What's more, they weren't teaching history. They weren't teaching much of anything at all, except how to be a liberal political activist.

Tom found this out firsthand during a memorable visit to the Tucson High Magnet School in 2006. Several weeks before, in a speech to the high school students, Dolores Huerta, a co-founder of the United Farm Workers, had charged that Republicans "hate Latinos." Tom was outraged and sent his aide, Margaret Garcia-Dugan, to the school to rebut this politically charged slander. Margaret only wanted students to move beyond generalities and look at realities. At a minimum, she expected them to hear her out. Instead the students, indoctrinated by their La Raza Studies teachers, turned their backs and walked out.

Tom wasn't going to sit idly by while hatred and intolerance were being taught in our public schools, and I was with him. These kids don't need political indoctrination at school; they need to learn to read, write, and speak English. They needed to learn real history, not political propaganda. They needed to be taught to understand and respect their fellow Americans, not hate and resent them. Tom and I deeply believe that we're not doing Mexican American kids any favors by neglecting traditional areas of study in favor of hip-hop lyrics and politically charged rhetoric.

That's why, in the midst of all the furor over SB 1070 in May 2010, I signed a bill that cut funds to school districts with ethnic studies programs that teach race hatred or the overthrow of the U.S. government. I was not going to allow Arizona's tax dollars to be spent on programs that tell some Arizona children that other Arizona children were their oppressors. My spokesman,

Paul Senseman, got it exactly right: "Governor Brewer signed the bill because she believes, and the legislation states, that public school students should be taught to treat and value each other as individuals and not be taught to resent or hate other races or classes of people."

In Arizona, we wear our Mexican and American Indian cultural traditions proudly. But it's one thing to learn and understand other cultures; it's another to deny that there is a set of values that define what it means to be American. And it is another thing entirely to teach your students to hate their country.

The irony of the whole situation is that in Europe, where multiculturalism has taken deep root, they're closer to understanding this than the Obama administration is. For decades, the English, French, and Germans, to name just a few, have pursued policies of multiculturalism that have actively encouraged their immigrant populations to retain their native countries' traditions and values. People who have advocated for a traditional "European" set of values have been accused of hate crimes. The result is immigrant communities in many parts of Europe that are backward, violent, and alienated. But some European leaders are finally realizing that tolerating intolerance in the name of tolerance is a fool's errand.

Prime Minister David Cameron of Great Britain gets it. "We have even tolerated these segregated communities behaving in ways that run counter to our values," he said at a security conference in Europe earlier this year. "So when a white person holds objectionable views—racism, for example—we rightly condemn them. But when equally unacceptable views or practices have come from someone who isn't white, we've been too cautious, frankly even fearful, to stand up to them."

Nicolas Sarkozy of France was pithier: "We have been too concerned about the identity of the person who was arriving and not enough about the identity of the country that was receiving him."

President Sarkozy is exactly right. In the end, the illegal immigration debate isn't about the identity of those coming to America; it's about preserving the identity of America itself.

The truth is that too many who don't want to secure our borders don't see America as anything special or worth fighting for. People talk a lot about something called "American exceptionalism" these days. It's a pretty misunderstood concept. It doesn't mean that, as Americans, we think we're better than the rest of the world. It means that we understand, care about, and cultivate the set of values that have made our nation exceptional—values like freedom, free enterprise, and religious tolerance. Those who don't believe in protecting America's borders generally don't believe that America is exceptional either. Quite the contrary; they see it as a place that needs to be radically changed—or "fundamentally transformed," in Barack Obama's words. They don't care about our identity—in fact, they see a strong, cohesive American identity as something people cling to out of bigotry and fear. They see being proud to be an American as an expression not of pride but of prejudice. They find it kind of embarrassing.

How else do you explain the Obama administration apologizing to China for something like SB 1070? And yet that's exactly what happened. A few weeks after I signed the law, Michael Posner, the assistant secretary for Democracy, Human Rights and Labor at the State Department, held a briefing regarding a U.S.-China human rights dialogue held that week. One of the members of the press asked whether SB 1070 had come up. Posner answered in the affirmative. Actually, he did more than that. "We brought it up early and often," he said. "It was mentioned in the first session and as a troubling trend in our society, and an indication that we have to deal with issues of discrimination or potential discrimination."

Posner's comments are very indicative of this elite liberal mentality. China is a routine human rights violator, torturing dissidents, crushing its own population. How little regard for America could Posner have to feel that he must actually *apologize* to a country like China for the law we passed in Arizona?

Later the Obama State Department included Arizona in its report to the United Nations Human Rights Council. The UNHRC is without a doubt the very worst of the UN bodies. It is a collection of thugs and dictators from such great human-rights-respecting nations as Libya, Cuba, Saudi Arabia, and China, whose main function is to pass hypocritical and obscene resolutions against Israel. What could lead the leaders of a great nation to give such people the power to pass judgment on the state of Arizona? How profoundly self-loathing can you get? And what is the real human rights violation? A law that enforces federal law while prohibiting racial profiling? Or allowing men, women, and children to be systematically tortured and abused by vicious thugs and gangsters?

We are a country of immigrants because we are the greatest values magnet in the history of mankind. To give away that power is a mistake of monumental proportions. We need more assimilation to American values, not less.

On July 28, 2010, just one day before SB 1070 was scheduled to go into effect, U.S. District Judge Susan Bolton ruled to prevent from being implemented the provisions of the law that allowed police to check immigration status and that criminalized the failure of immigrants to carry proof of legal status. Like the lawsuit itself, Judge Bolton's ruling piled implausibility on top of implausibility to construct its case. She worried that legal immigrants from visa-waiver countries such as Sweden and Singapore might suffer under the law, even though the proof of their legal status is right there on their passports. She worried that lawful applicants for asylum who hadn't received their paperwork would be "harassed." And she laughably concluded that the DHS clearinghouse that verifies immigrants' legal status would be overwhelmed with inquiries. Really?

As someone who has lived in Arizona for forty years, I can assure Judge Bolton that the last thing our police are interested in doing is harassing innocent Swedes and Singaporeans. The last thing they want to do is "harass" anyone. Moreover, our problem is not asylum seekers who don't yet have their paperwork engaging in high-speed shoot-outs on our freeways or torturing people in drop houses. Our problems dwell in the real world.

But for many of our old friends in the unions and the liberal activist groups, I think Judge Bolton's ruling was more of a letdown than a victory. They had buses gassed up in California ready to ship in hundreds of protesters when the law was implemented. Liberal immigration groups had called for yet another "national day of action." A protest march was planned across the Brooklyn Bridge, among other acts of outrage, when the law actually went into effect. When Judge Bolton blocked its implementation, you could practically feel the fund-raising and recruiting efforts drying up.

It was then that it dawned on me: If the Obama administration and the unions and the civil rights groups didn't have

SB 1070 to rail against, they would have had to make it up. The law fit their purposes to a T. They could rally their base by calling us names and get everyone excited before the election. And they could generate lots of noise to mask the fact that they weren't doing one constructive thing to solve our immigration crisis.

There's just one thing standing in the way of the open-border left: the people. The people of Arizona and America at large don't agree with its agenda. They don't buy the demonization of opponents and can see through their rhetorical smokescreen. After my serious rivals dropped out of the Republican primary, I faced a tough fight against Terry Goddard for the right to remain governor in 2010. My critics have accused me of "riding" the popularity of SB 1070 to reelection. And while it's true that SB 1070 has remained very popular despite what may be the greatest campaign of political and media distortion in our history, the law wasn't the key to my eventual victory; it was the issue the law represents that was the key.

Washington is lying to America when it comes to the border, and Americans know it. What we want—what the voters of Arizona want—is someone who will stand up to the bullies of the left and honestly represent the people. Whether it's the fight against Obamacare or the fight to secure the border, fewer and fewer people are buying the "Washington knows best" routine. I took on this fight. It was bruising and ugly. It's not one I ever, ever want to repeat. But nineteen months later, I'm still smiling. Why? Because (to quote the president) *I won*. Yes, I won the election, but I also won an even greater prize. My fellow Arizonans and the people of this great and good country still stand with me.

CONCLUSION

On January 8, 2011, I was with my longtime friend and communications director Paul Senseman, my chief of staff, Eileen Klein, and my speechwriter, Mark Genrich, in the House chamber at the Arizona Capitol. Other staff members, like Kim Sabow, Brian McNeil, Joe Kanefield, and Colin Shipley, were with me. We were doing our final walk-through for my State of the State address, scheduled for just two days later. There was a lot of anticipation for the new year. My inaugural had been five days before, and I was preparing to roll out a big agenda in my upcoming speech.

We had paused in the members' lounge following our survey of the chamber when phones began to ring and BlackBerrys beeped. I was reviewing my speech. When I looked up, I saw my staff huddled together. They looked shocked. Paul called me over and said they had some very bad news. He had just received a call from Bobby Halliday, my director of the Department of Public Safety. There had been a shooting in Tucson. Several people had been shot, including a judge and Gabby Giffords.

I don't remember how long I stood there trying to process what I had just heard. I consider Gabby a friend. She is one of the most genuine, most sincere people I have ever known. We had worked together when I was secretary of state and she was in the State Senate. Gabby represented part of our southern border in the Eighth Congressional District. She knew, as I did, the people who live and work down there, people who are suffering because of the federal government's negligence. We stood on different sides of the political aisle and we did not agree on SB 1070, but we had stood side by side in calling on Washington to do its job to secure our border.

My first thought was, *What can we do?* I went into action. Get me the mayor of Tucson on the phone. I need to speak with my director of DPS. We need to verify the information we've received.

My second thought was that this must be the work of a madman. I flashed back to fourteen years earlier, when a colleague on the Maricopa County Board of Supervisors was shot in the hallway while exiting the auditorium where we had just had a board meeting. I remembered hearing the loud crack and smelling the odor of the fired weapon as it filled the auditorium. I remembered screaming as I ducked under a table for safety and then tried to figure our where the rest of my colleagues were and whether they were safe. When it was over, the board member survived, thank goodness. The shooter, a homeless man, was convicted of attempted first-degree murder. It rattled everyone and forced us to beef up security in government buildings.

I stayed in the House chamber as we contacted federal, state, and local officials and watched the coverage from Tucson. The news was reporting that Gabby was dead, although nothing official had been reported to me.

The reports revealed that it had been a sunny Saturday at a supermarket. Gabby was doing her duty as a public servant, meeting with the citizens she represented. It was something we all did in Arizona. We called them supermarket Saturdays. We would go out and spend the day talking to our constituents. If you couldn't find a supermarket, you went to a park or even a parking lot. But we had always been proud of the fact that we kept in close touch with the people we represented. And we had never been afraid. Until now.

The news came in a rush. At some point, after what felt like an hour but could have been less, we got word that Gabby wasn't dead but was gravely wounded and being taken to University Medical Center in Tucson. Still, the news was almost unfathomably grim. U.S. District Judge John Roll had also been shot. Six people were confirmed dead, including a nine-year-old girl. Thirteen people had been wounded.

We're a small political community in Arizona. We all knew Gabby or members of her staff. We all had friends in Tucson. Mayor Bob Walkup had served on my transition team. I had relatives in Tucson, and my son Michael had graduated from the University of Arizona. As the news got worse and worse, our sense of helplessness grew deeper and deeper. Then, as though it were the most natural thing in the world to do—as if it were the *only* thing to do—Paul, Eileen, Mark, the other staffers, and I silently formed a circle right there in the members' lounge of the House chamber. We took each other's hands, and we prayed. We prayed for the victims. We prayed for the Arizonans who were responding to the tragedy. We prayed for our state and for our country. We prayed that the peace that had been robbed from us that morning would not be long in returning.

I spent the next several hours in the House chamber. I received phone calls and security briefings from Secretary Napolitano, FBI Director Robert Mueller, and Public Safety director Halliday. A couple of hours into the tragedy, Eileen told me the president was on the telephone. I went into the House Speaker's conference room to take the call. President Obama was very gracious. He had stepped out of the Situation Room in the White House to update me. He shared with me the information he had from the FBI. It was from the president that I first learned that Judge Roll was dead. It was a heartbreaking but heartening call. It was the first time I had spoken to the president in which there was no party, no politics, no agenda. We were just two human beings, two Americans, brought together by a hideous, unnecessary, incomprehensible tragedy. He pledged to do everything he could to bring the shooter to justice. I thanked him sincerely for his call and hung up.

I knew that the president would be making a televised statement, and out of respect I chose to wait until he was finished before I addressed the press. Many people earlier that day had eagerly jumped to be on the air without really having any information. I knew, however, that Arizonans would be looking to me for comfort and strength.

We watched the president give his remarks from the White House, then I went outside and met with the press. I could barely keep it together. I asked the people of Arizona and the people of America to keep the victims and their families in their prayers. After I had made my brief statement, the second question I received from the assembled reporters was about how I felt the shooting reflected on the state of Arizona. I answered honestly: It certainly didn't reflect favorably on our state. But our people are overwhelmingly good and decent, I said. Tragedies happen, and what we needed to do was to make sure the perpetrators were held accountable.

We were less than forty-eight hours away from the historic opening of the fiftieth session of the Arizona legislature. I had planned to use my State of the State address to announce an ambitious new agenda to create jobs, improve education, and reform taxes. But none of that seemed appropriate now. So I spent the next day, a Sunday, rewriting my remarks with my staff. There would be a time for policy; now was the time for grieving and trying to begin to heal.

In the end my address was short—less than ten minutes. I called for prayers and comfort for the victims and their families. I led the chamber in a moment of silence. And after we had humbled ourselves to seek God's guidance and his strength, I felt the need to also be defiant. When we opened our eyes and lifted our heads from our moment of silent prayer, I looked at the legislators, the dignitaries, the judges, and the other constitutional officers who faced me in the chamber and I thought of all the people who now looked to us to ensure that justice would be served.

I paraphrased Isaiah: "I believe Arizona will rise on wings like eagles," I said. "We will run and not get weary. We will walk and not grow weak."

My voice rose. "Arizona is in pain," I concluded. "Yes, our grief is profound. We are yet in the first hours of our sorrow. But we have not been brought down."

I paused. "We will never be brought down." The chamber rose in thunderous applause.

I had meant every word.

The sun had yet to set on Arizona on the day of Gabby's shooting when the hate talk began again. This time it came from a disappointing source: Democratic Pima County sheriff Clarence Dupnik. In an interview with the Tucson NBC affiliate that was aired live on MSNBC just hours after the shooting, Sheriff Dupnik proceeded to light a flame that would burn out of control for the next few weeks.

"I want to tell you right now that people like myself are very, very angry at what's going on in our country, and I think that it's time that we take a look at what kind of hatred that we inflame by all the crap that goes on," he said. He clearly meant to imply, without a shred of evidence, that the shootings had been politically motivated.

"When you look at unbalanced people, how they respond to the vitriol that comes out of certain mouths about tearing down the government, the anger, the hatred, the bigotry that goes on in this country is getting to be outrageous," Dupnik elaborated at a news conference later that evening. "And unfortunately, Arizona has become sort of the capital. We have become the mecca for prejudice and bigotry."

At seventy-three, Sheriff Dupnik had served seven terms. He was a well-known political liberal who had already declared that he would not enforce SB 1070 because it was a "racist" law. He was entitled to state his views about SB 1070, but these comments were beyond the pale. The grief we felt was raw. We were hurting for people and families we knew and cared about. And here this craven opportunist was exploiting our shared tragedy to score a cheap political point. I couldn't believe it. And of course, Dupnik's comments from the scene in Tucson were all that the liberal mainstream media needed to unleash their residual bias against Arizona.

That night, MSNBC's Keith Olbermann praised Sheriff Dupnik's words and brazenly linked the shooting to a year-old

Sarah Palin Web site that used crosshairs to identify Gabby's district as one of twenty vulnerable Democratic districts in the 2010 elections. Olbermann called for any Republican who wouldn't acknowledge that Palin's map was responsible for the Tucson shooting to be expelled from public office. "This morning in Arizona, this age in which this country would accept 'targeting' of political opponents and putting bull's-eyes over their faces and of the dangerous blurring between political rallies and guns shows, ended," Olbermann said, with his characteristic restraint and brevity. It was unsubstantiated. It was outrageous. And unfortunately, it was merely a taste of things to come.

It didn't seem to matter, when the facts came in, that the shooter was clearly a deeply unbalanced young man with no discernible political beliefs or agenda. The crazed look in his eyes as he stared at the cameras spoke volumes. Yet as the days went by, liberal journalists and politicos repeatedly accused Arizonans, gun owners, the Tea Party, and supporters of SB 1070 of being accomplices to mass murder. Each of them used Sheriff Dupnik's irresponsible comments as an excuse. The *New York Times* editorialized:

> It is legitimate to hold Republicans and particularly their most virulent supporters in the media responsible for the gale of anger that has produced the vast majority of these threats, setting the nation on edge. Many on the right have exploited the arguments of division, reaping political power by demonizing immigrants, or welfare recipients, or bureaucrats. They seem to have persuaded many Americans that the government is not just misguided, but the enemy of the people.
>
> That whirlwind has touched down most forcefully in Arizona . . .

After the furor over SB 1070 had subsided, the mainstream media and liberal politicians were now using a tragic event to wrongly smear Arizona again. After it turned out the facts did not support their argument, they simply turned to an argument for "civility" which was code for conservatives shutting up over Obamacare, immigration, and the Second Amendment, among other issues.

It's difficult to describe how painful it was to have to endure this kind of rhetoric—which accused me and my state of responsibility for the murders—while at the same time praying for the injured and mourning the lost. Gabby Giffords was fighting for her life. Arizona had lost Judge Roll. The Green family had lost their nine-year-old girl, Christina. The families of Dot Morris, Phyllis Schneck, Dorwan Stoddard, and Gabe Zimmerman no longer had their loved ones. That was where our hearts and our minds were. To play political games with our grief was unforgivable. But these people who posed as sober and responsible journalists saw the tragedy as an opportunity to be exploited. They were obscenely excited and thrilled by it.

Three days after the shooting, I traveled to the hospital in Tucson to meet with some of the wounded and their families. I couldn't see Gabby, but I met with Gabby's mother and her husband, Mark. I visited with Ron Barber and Pamela Simon, two congressional staff members who had been shot. And I met with Mavanelle Stoddard, whose husband, Dorwan, had given his life shielding her from the bullet fire.

I also had the opportunity to meet with the amazing men and women of the University of Arizona Medical Center, including Dr. Peter Rhee and Dr. Michael Lemole. I actually met with the entire team that was on duty during the crisis, including the staffers who were cleaning the rooms between caring for the victims. Dr. Rhee described the setting to me as "a war scene . . . the closet to battle that we could get." I was so proud of everyone at the University Medical Center. They showed remarkable skill and poise at a chaotic time. I thought how, if I or any of my family ever had a life-threatening emergency, God forbid, I want it to be in Tucson.

The tragedy was weighing heavily on my heart before I visited the hospital. The shock and grief had taken their toll. But I left feeling surprisingly better. There was such hope there, and such resilience. It was humbling and energizing at the same time. I had gone to Tucson thinking I would try to comfort the wounded and their families. In the end, they had comforted me.

On the day after my visit to the hospital, there was a memorial for the victims at the McKale Memorial Center on the University of Arizona campus. It pains me to say it, but I was more uplifted by the first event than the second. My experience at the University Medical Center in Tucson comforted and inspired me. My experience at the memorial shocked and disappointed me.

Jan Lesher, Janet Napolitano's former chief of staff and the campaign manager of my Democratic challenger for governor, Terry Goddard, coordinated a lot of the logistics for the service. From the start, it took on the air of a pep rally more than a memorial service. The choice of venue, I thought, was a particularly bad one. The McKale Center is the home of the Arizona Wildcats. It seats more than 14,000 spectators, and it was so full that night that an overflow of another 13,000 spectators were at the adjacent football stadium. The sheer number of people, as well as the large number of students, made it all but inevitable that the event would come off as more celebratory than somber. University officials seemed to encourage that by doing things like handing out more than $60,000 worth of T-shirts to people entering the arena. I know the audience's heart was in the right place. I know everyone was there to show love and respect for the victims. But it was too soon for the kind of raucous event the memorial turned into. In a few weeks or months, we could have had a cheering, boisterous tribute to both the heroes and the victims of the shooting. But not four days after the tragedy.

I had the honor of traveling to Davis-Monthan Air Force Base to meet President and Mrs. Obama when they arrived for the event. Mrs. Obama couldn't have been more gracious and friendly. I was sick that we had to meet again under such circumstances.

After the President and First Lady walked down the steps of Air Force One, a steady stream of other dignitaries from Washington followed. The entire Arizona congressional delegation was there, as well as other members of Congress and members of the cabinet. Before the memorial began in the McKale Center, we waited in the lobby of the Wildcat offices. I talked with FBI Director Mueller and again thanked him for his help. Retired Supreme Court justice and Arizona native Sandra Day O'Connor introduced me to Justice Anthony Kennedy. Representative Nancy Pelosi was very gracious and introduced me to her daughter, who lives in Scottsdale. I spoke as well with Senators McCain and Kyl, and Florida representative Debbie Wasserman Schultz introduced herself.

We walked into the memorial expecting a serious, respectful scene. From the get-go, the event was something different. As I sat in the audience, next to the man who was even then engaged in suing me—Attorney General Eric Holder—I listened with tears in my eyes to the tributes to the Arizonans who had made themselves heroes that day. I respectfully watched as Daniel Hernández, who likely saved Representative Gifford's life at the scene of the shooting, rejected the title "hero" and insisted it be reserved for "those who deserve it."

Still, the loud cheers from the audience bothered me. They struck the wrong note for a memorial.

When it was my turn to speak, I thanked the president and Mrs. Obama, Secretary Napolitano, Attorney General Holder, and the other Washington officials who were there. "Your presence today reminds us that we are not alone with our sorrow," I said. "America grieves with us." I made a point of mentioning every one of the shooting victims by name. But when I mentioned the youngest victim, Christina-Taylor Green, the stadium oddly erupted in cheers and applause. It caught me off guard. I remember looking out at the audience in confusion. What were they applauding? Looking back, I know how the cheers and applause were intended—as a tribute to Christina—but at the time it seemed profoundly out of place. I guess that's just what happens when you hold a memorial service in an arena full of boisterous students instead of in a smaller, more intimate setting.

Much was said and written about President Obama's speech that evening. He has been praised for offering a healing message that night, and rightly so. We were mourning six dead Arizonans and praying for more than a dozen wounded. We were hailing the heroes of that morning. It was only right that we put politics aside, that we not point fingers of blame, that we be civil and respectful of one another. We were all moved when he exhorted us to discuss our differences "with a good dose of humility."

"Rather than pointing fingers or assigning blame," President Obama said, "let us use this occasion to expand our moral imaginations, to listen to each other more carefully."

The president's words stayed with me. They were the basis of what became known as the "Tucson truce"—a supposed end to the name calling and bitterness that had marked the tragedy so far. I liked the idea. But I wondered how long it would last.

In the weeks and months that followed the tragedy, Arizona healed as Gabby made her inspiring recovery. Things seemed to settle down for a while. The truce seemed to be holding.

In February, I took the bold step of filing a countersuit against the federal government for failing to uphold its constitutional and statutory obligations to secure the national border. Ever since the Obama administration had sued us over SB 1070, Arizonans had been coming up to me and suggesting that we sue the federal government right back. I weighed that option, and my legal advisers began preparing a countersuit. They thought it was important that if the administration's lawsuit went all the way to the Supreme Court, our claims would go with it. A countersuit ensured that would happen, and when we finally got a decision, it would settle once and for all the matter of the federal government's responsibility to secure the border.

So on February 11, 2011, I filed the suit. "Because the federal government has failed to protect the citizens of Arizona," I announced to catcalls and jeers from protesters at a press conference outside the federal courthouse in Phoenix, "I am left with no other choice."

In April, almost a year after I had signed the controversial bill and more than eight months since Judge Bolton had issued the injunction against parts of SB 1070, the Ninth Circuit issued its ruling on our appeal. A three-judge panel of the court upheld Judge Bolton's injunction, and our appeal failed. No surprises here. This was the same court that had ruled the words "under God" in the Pledge of Allegiance unconstitutional in 2002. So rather than get the same result by having the full Ninth Circuit rule on the injunction, we decided to take our case directly to the Supreme Court.

Since the high court had already heard arguments for the term that would end in June 2011, we knew our best shot to have our case heard would be in the fall term, which began in October. There was always the possibility, of course, that the court would decline to hear our case, but we figured we had a couple of things going in our favor. First was the weakness of the Obama administration's case against us. It was based on faulty hypotheticals and a deliberate misreading of the law. Second was the fact that the principle behind SB 1070—states enforcing federal immigration law when the federal government won't—was spreading like wildfire across the country.

In the year following the passage of SB 1070, similar laws were introduced in California, Colorado, Florida, Iowa, Kansas, Kentucky, Maine, Michigan, Mississippi, Nebraska, New Hampshire, North Carolina, South Dakota, Tennessee, and Wyoming. Indiana and Oklahoma also had similar bills advance through their legislatures. And in Georgia, South Carolina, Utah, and Alabama, SB 1070–like laws were passed and signed into law.

What the proliferation of such copycat laws in states across the country said to us was that we weren't alone in being fed up with the failure of the federal government to control illegal immigration. Of course, in many of these states, as in Arizona, these laws are being held up by legal challenges. This makes it time—past time, really—for the Supreme Court to rule and hopefully put an end to the anti-democratic strategy of using the courts to overrule the duly enacted wishes of the people.

In May, I got some good news when the Supreme Court upheld Arizona's 2007 law enforcing federal law concerning employment of illegal aliens. The court ruled that our employer-sanctions law does not conflict with federal law and is therefore constitutional. SB 1070 and our employer-sanctions law are obviously different, but the court has acknowledged that there is a legitimate role for the states to play in combating illegal immigration. I took it as a hopeful sign that the court would take the same position when it comes to laws like SB 1070.

While I am very hopeful that the high court will take up our appeal of the injunction against parts of SB 1070, I also understand that the Court considers relatively few cases each year. Up to now, all we have been in court about is whether all the provisions of SB 1070 can be enforced while the law is litigated. If the Supreme Court does not review the injunction, the fight is far from over. We will simply go back to the U.S. District Court and start the trial on the merits for the disputed portions of SB 1070. Lost in all the media confusion is the fact that the many important provisions of SB 1070 have not been blocked by the courts—such as the prohibitions against hiring day laborers, "sanctuary" cities, and the transportation of illegal aliens. Even more important than SB 1070, we can elect a president next year that will work with the states, rather than sue them and stand with foreign nations against them in federal courts, to enforce federal immigration laws and at last truly secure our border. Our law was born out of frustration with a federal government that won't do its job. The fight will not end until the federal government does that job.

During the first few months of 2011, the federal government seemed to revert to its typical indifference to the issue of illegal immigration. Then, in April, the Obama White House convened an unusual group of participants to talk about the issue. A strange cast of characters—everyone from the Reverend Al Sharpton to Hollywood actress Eva Longoria to former California governor Arnold Schwarzenegger to AFL-CIO president Richard Trumka—was invited, but not one sitting governor and not one current member of Congress. I told the press that I considered it a "snub" that I wasn't invited. Not that I was so eager to return to the Obama White House and be lectured again— been there, done that. But I could have added a perspective that is sorely missing when the likes of Al Sharpton and Richard Trumka gather around the policy table. For me and the people I represent, immigration policy affects our daily lives. For them, such real-world concerns take a backseat to politics. But maybe that was the point of the meeting.

The media was full of speculation that President Obama was making a play for Hispanic voters. When he ran for president, he had promised those voters that he would aggressively push for comprehensive immigration reform during the first year of his presidency. But like so much else that he promised to do, such as closing Gitmo and healing the planet, it didn't happen. Even while Obama's party controlled the Senate and the House by historic margins, he did nothing about immigration. Latino voters were upset, the theory went, and the president was attempting to, if not make good on his promise, then at least look as if he *really, really wanted* to do so, if only it weren't for those racist Republicans.

Buzz began to build about a trip to the Southwest that Obama planned for May—his first official visit to the southwestern border as president. The word was that he would deliver a major speech on immigration in El Paso and then head off to a series of fund-raisers in Texas for his 2012 campaign. Beyond that, no one really knew what he was planning. The Republican leadership in the House complained that there'd been no outreach from the White House on the immigration issue. All they would say was that he was "trying to lead a constructive and civil debate on America's broken immigration system."

I watched the president's El Paso speech while sitting at my desk at the State Capitol. At first he spoke movingly about America—in words that I couldn't agree with more. "In embracing America, you can *become* American," he said. "That is what makes this country great. That enriches all of us."

With his next words, though, as he so often does, the president took a demagogic turn. He talked about how it's easier for politicians to defer fixing our immigration system until the next election. "And there's always a next election." True that! But did he realize he was talking about himself? Not only that, but we in Arizona *had* done something about illegal immigration. We didn't wait for an election. And what did he do? He sued us for having the courage of our convictions!

President Obama next tried to make the case that immigration reform was good for the economy—I guess he thought he would kill two election issues with one stone. Immigration fuels innovation and job creation, he said. Intel, Google, eBay—all had been founded by immigrants. That's great, I thought, but what does this have to do with the drug cartels on the border? The shoot-outs on our freeways? The invasion of our suburbs? The skyrocketing health, education, and incarceration costs? How does this rhetoric help us?

In a section of the speech that would prove to be great fodder for fact-checkers, the president tried to highlight everything his administration had done to secure the border. They'd doubled the number of Border Patrol agents, he said. (Actually, the Bush administration had done most of that.) They'd "basically complete[d]" the border fence. (Actually, the GAO had just reported that less than half the border was under "operational control"—of the government, that is.) I noticed that when the president mentioned the fence, his audience in El Paso booed. "Tear it down!" someone yelled.

Then the president seemed to get a little angry. "We have gone above and beyond what was requested by the very Republicans who said they supported broader reform as long as we got serious about enforcement," he said. "All the stuff they asked for, we've done. But even though we've answered these concerns, I've got to say I suspect that there are still going to be some who are going to try to move the goalposts on us one more time." Some in the crowd shouted, "They're racist!"

Then the president's tone became mocking. "They're going to say we need to quadruple the Border Patrol. Or they'll need a higher fence. Maybe they'll need a moat. Maybe they'll want alligators in the moat. They'll never be satisfied, and I understand. That's politics."

Moats? Alligators? Politics?? With these calculated remarks, Obama was dismissing our concerns as essentially groundless— mere political grandstanding. He was making clear that in his view, the entire controversy about the border had been ginned up to polarize the electorate and win votes for the Republicans. If anything, this was a case of classic Freudian projection, since that's precisely what he and his allies in Congress and the press had been doing, even cynically exploiting the shootings in Tucson. Was this what Obama considered a "constructive and civil debate"? *I'd hate to see him when he decides to be uncivil*, I thought.

Not even the mainstream media outlets could bring themselves to defend the speech on policy grounds. NBC political director Chuck Todd tweeted after the speech, "Of all the O's appearances on the road that were NOT fundraisers, this #immigration speech has most campaign feel to it yet." It was the most disappointing conceivable outcome to the truce we'd embarked on four months earlier. The president hadn't just been uncivil; he had been unconstructively so. He hadn't done anything to secure the border. He hadn't advanced the cause of immigration reform. All he had done was condescend to American Hispanics by assuming that they could be bought off by an empty, cynically polarizing speech. All he had done was mock people who know—because we live it every day—that he'd not done nearly enough to secure the border. All he'd done was further divide Congress and the American people by blaming his political opponents for his own undeniable inaction. I called it his "promise something, do nothing, blame someone" political spin from Washington, D.C.

It was one of the most cynical political acts I had seen in almost thirty years of public life.

So much for hope and change.

Our problems were greatly compounded in August 2011, while Congress was on summer recess and President Obama was on his Martha's Vineyard vacation, when Janet Napolitano announced the administration's plan to "review" 300,000 illegal alien deportation cases. The review would be based on nineteen guidelines, many of which came straight out of the DREAM Act, which Congress had already refused to pass. Napolitano dressed this up as "prioritizing" the federal government's resources against aliens who are criminals or pose a threat to national security or public safety. This went right along with the memorandum that ICE director John Morton had issued in June, instructing agents on how to use "discretion" when deporting illegal aliens.

Let's call this what it is: backdoor amnesty for hundreds of thousands, if not millions, of illegal aliens.

President Obama is encouraging more illegal immigration by telling illegal aliens they won't be deported as long as they don't commit a crime or overstay their visa. By doing so, he is making fools out of all the law-abiding immigrants who do obey our laws. Most important, he is effectively saying that our nation does not get to decide who enters and stays in our country—the illegal aliens do.

Just three weeks earlier, in a speech before the Council of La Raza, President Obama had rejected the call to bypass Congress and implement immigration reform on his own. He said, "I know some people want me to bypass Congress and change the laws on my own. And, believe me, right now, dealing with Congress, the idea of doing things on my own is very tempting. . . . But that's not how our system works. That's not how our democracy functions. That's not how our Constitution is written."

Obama got it right in his speech and really got it wrong three weeks later. By implementing immigration reform on his own, he is violating the rule of law. President Obama needs to remember that we elected a president who serves under the law, and did not anoint a king who is above it.

You see, the broken campaign promises of 2008 are really making immigration a difficult topic for President Obama in 2012. Originally, candidate Obama had promised that he would make comprehensive immigration reform a top priority during his first year as president. But once in office, with a Democratic majority in the House and Senate, he made Obamacare the top priority. Comprehensive immigration reform quickly became a talking point as a "second-term" issue. Now, with his poll numbers plummeting, especially among Latino voters, President Obama is pandering to a key constituency and trying to redeem his broken promise by executive fiat.

After the announcement of Obama's backdoor amnesty plan, I posted a press release on my Facebook page denouncing it. I also included Linda Eddy's poster of me as Rosie the Riveter, flexing my muscles, next to the words ARIZONA: DOING THE JOB THE FEDS WON'T DO! Within hours I had over 10,000 "likes" and comments. This was one of the largest responses I had ever received on Facebook. As I went to bed that night, I wondered how much the response would grow by morning.

Unfortunately, I'll never know. Because Facebook censored the post.

The next morning, the post was missing. Not until I read my e-mail did I know exactly what had happened. Facebook had e-mailed me at 5:12 A.M. telling me that the photo I had posted along with my comments violated their community standards.

Really? That image? The one I had been using on my Facebook page for more than a year? It didn't make sense.

So I did what I thought was right. I reposted the statement and image with an explanation that Facebook had censored my first post. That set off a firestorm. I received over 35,000 "likes" and comments that afternoon, and the media was all over the story. Facebook later apologized, claiming the post was removed "in error."

In the midst of my campaign for governor, I made a statement about law enforcement finding beheaded bodies in the desert. My political opponent and the mainstream media quickly pounced on the claim, saying that Arizona coroners couldn't find any evidence of headless bodies having been found. I was, of course, trying to make the larger point about the uncontrolled, drug-fueled violence on the border region, giving the impression that we'd found headless bodies in our desert, the Arizona desert, when what I meant was that we didn't want that sort of depraved violence to spill over into our own towns and cities. All that the media and my political opponents could talk about, of course, was how I had misspoken. The ongoing suffering and horrific violence on the border—the point I was trying to make—was completely ignored.

I thought about all the fun the media had had with that story recently when I saw a report that the bodies of eight decapitated men had been dumped along the road in Durango, Mexico. It was the second find of decapitated bodies that week. Earlier, eleven headless bodies had been discovered, six of them strategically placed across the street from a middle school.

When I see these kinds of reports, I worry about how history will judge us. Mexico is on the verge of collapse. Almost 40,000 of its citizens have been murdered in the drug wars there. And despite the desperate claims of the administration to the contrary, the violence of these wars is coming to America. What our national leaders have offered in response is a do-nothing policy cloaked in blame shifting and name calling. The president promised action in his first year in office. When he failed to deliver on that, his only response was to point fingers of blame. To please his rabid political base, he accuses those who want the border secured of racism and other ugly motives. For the majority of Americans who want the border secure, he blames Republicans for his failure to act. It's all an elaborate Kabuki theater designed to conceal a concerted policy of doing nothing.

Securing the border isn't rocket science. We've already made great strides in California and Texas. As I said at the beginning, border control can be achieved. To deal with the illegal traffic that these partial solutions have channeled into Arizona, we need to do a few relatively simple things.

We need a real border fence, particularly where the traffic is heaviest, along the Tucson sector of our border.

We need a robust National Guard that sticks around to get the job done.

We need to reimburse border states for the costs illegal aliens place on them, especially in terms of incarceration.

And, of course, we need to enforce our laws against illegal immigration. We need to send the message to would-be crossers that the risk of death and torture that is so frequently associated with illegal immigration just isn't worth it. We need to send the message to people in other countries—and our own—that we take our laws seriously. That we honor them. That we enforce them fairly, without regard to the color of one's skin or the accent of one's voice.

This is what we've tried to do in Arizona. And we've run into a buzz saw of unions, liberal activists, civil rights groups, and the Obama reelection campaign. The virulence of their reaction has been eye-opening, to say the least. I know now that I could have spent half a year refining SB 1070 to add protection after protection against racial profiling and it wouldn't have made a lick of difference. This isn't a battle about immigration. It's a battle about something much bigger.

I keep coming back to the Krentz family's statement after Rob was murdered.

"We hold no malice toward the Mexican people for this senseless act but do hold the political forces in this country and Mexico accountable for what has happened."

The Obama administration and the liberal media have been in overdrive since I signed SB 1070 to portray people like the Krentzes—people who support the law and support enforcing all our immigration laws—as racists. But Rob Krentz wasn't a racist. He had compassion for the illegal crossers who were trashing his land and sapping his livelihood and who probably killed him.

Since I signed SB 1070, the media and the lawyers in the White House and the federal courts have been full of talk about justice for immigrants, both legal and illegal. I've listened as judges have opined about fairness for Swedes in America who didn't have documentation of their legal status and asylum applicants who haven't received their paperwork yet. But where is the justice for the Krentz family? They looked to their government for safety and all they got was silence. They said there was a problem and were told by an arrogant Washington that they didn't know what they were talking about. Rob died, and they were accused of exaggerating the problem for political ends. Where is the justice in that?

They say America is a place that is always in the process of becoming, a country that is never finished. I think that's largely true. Legal immigration is one of the things that keeps America vibrant and innovative. My vision of the border is one that is safe and accessible. It's one that fosters trade and free enterprise and cultural exchange. We need to preserve and protect legal immigration in America.

America keeps changing, but there are some American values that are concrete and timeless. The Krentz family embodies these values. They are hardworking, caring for their neighbors, and committed to their communities. All they want from their government—all Rob wanted—is to be left alone to work their land in safety and security. That's all. But they rightly acknowledged that there are forces on both sides of the border that won't let them do that.

I keep returning to the Krentz family's statement because I worry about what motivates the forces they referred to. I wonder whether they share the same vision of America that Rob had— that I have and I think most Americans have. Multiculturalists will deny it, but being an American means something. It means embracing American values. It means being free to create your own destiny. It means respecting the freedom of your fellow Americans to do the same. It carries responsibilities as well as rights.

I ran into Sue Krentz recently and she gave me a key charm she had been wearing since shortly after Rob was killed. For her, it was a loving and, I think, hopeful gesture. She said she had worn it to remind herself to pray to Saint Anthony, the saint not only of lost things but of miracles.

"I want you to find the person who invaded my life and ruined my safe haven," she told me. "Because if they are willing to kill someone like Rob—minding his own business on his own land—then we are all in danger."

Sue prays for justice for her husband, safety for her family, and security for her country. Her family, which has been through so much, harbors no ill will toward law-abiding people of any color or nationality. They reserve their anger and contempt for the criminals who have invaded their lives, and the governments that are unwilling to do anything about them.

This, in the end, is what the debate over SB 1070 is really about: whether we honor families like the Krentzes, who want some measure of control over their lives, or whether we surrender to an arrogant and arbitrary federal government.

Let me settle the debate: We are a free and striving people, not the subjects of an overbearing government. Call me biased, but I believe this is true in Arizona more than just about anyplace else. We used to be a country that was proud to assert that. These days, you get called names for saying such a thing. But if our critics have learned one thing by now, it's that we can take it. We won't be intimidated, and we won't back down. So bring on the scorpions. And God bless the USA.

Acknowledgments

I can say without hesitation that I'm glad this exercise of writing the book has come to an end. The writing, the interviews, the research, the photo selection, and the editing have been a lot of work. More than I first imagined!

To begin, I'll acknowledge those who made this book possible. Thank you, Roger, for all your hard work from the very beginning. I truly appreciate everyone who supported my efforts: my agent, Mel Berger, and everyone at Broadside Books and HarperCollins, including Jonathan Burnham, Adam Bellow, Kathryn Whitenight, Tina Andreadis, and others who helped with the book. I'm deeply grateful for Jessica Gavora and the excellent job she did in helping me share the truth about SB 1070, the immigration crisis, the liberal media, and union influences that Arizona and our country face. And, Michael—thank you for your diligence and for working with everyone throughout the entire process to make this happen.

This book would have never happened without the influence of my family. Let me begin with my parents, Wilford and Edna Drinkwine, who gave me unconditional love, guidance, and a strong sense of security. They taught me American values, pride in my country, and the importance of patriotism. My brother, Paul, who mercilessly teased me growing up and constantly challenged me, helped make me tough and strong. He held me accountable for my actions and taught me that my word is my bond. Thank you for your sense of humor, fun spirit, and always being there throughout my life. Thanks also for the steadfast support from my sister-in-law, Petra, who came to America legally!

My journey in life would not be the same without my loving husband, John, who has always encouraged and supported me. Thank you for never holding me back and for stretching me. Ron, John, and Michael are God's greatest gifts to me. My three boys taught me unconditional love, patience, sacrifice, and that there is always a different side to a story. I'm also grateful for my extended family and all of my nieces and nephews.

I'm indebted to staff who have helped me through all the battles—beginning with Kevin Tyne, who arrived with me at the governor's office, facing an almost impossible task. I know Arizona is also grateful for Eileen Klein's sacrifice to serve our state. Her energy, steady hand, decisive decision making, and judgment have made an enormous difference to our state. She doesn't ask anyone to do anything that she wouldn't do herself. And where would I be without my loyal and ready combatant and warrior, Richard Bark? I've been able to count on you, RB II, since you were an intern with me in the state senate.

I wouldn't have been able to survive the media onslaught without those on my communications team. Paul Senseman's ever-present smile and contagious laugh always brightened the toughest days. Thank you, Kim Sabow, for keeping me focused, organized, calm, and collected and above all making me feel comfortable.

I want to recognize my legal counsel, Joe Kanefield, who faces every challenge with an upbeat attitude and who has provided me with solid legal advice for the past eight years. I want to also thank John Bouma and the legal team at Snell and Wilmer for stepping up and defending Arizona.

I'm not sure what I'd do without Susie, who is my sounding board. I appreciate her always kind and sweet attitude, no matter the circumstances.

Thanks to the rest of my team, including Scott Smith, Brian McNeil, John Arnold, Tim Bee, Colin Shipley, Kelsey Bullington, Page Gonzales, Mark Genrich, and others in my administration, and to Tom Manos for his service to our state during very difficult times. I also want to acknowledge all those in my constituent services who have been inundated with thousands of phone calls, e-mails, and letters.

I'm extremely grateful to my DPS director, Bobby Halliday, and to all of the DPS officers who keep us safe on a daily basis. I appreciate Mike Bush and everyone on my security detail— Brian, Bob, Danny, Kevin, Kristi, Mark, Pete, Randy, Ray, Roger, Stanley, Scott, and Todd—for their professionalism and for keeping me and my family safe during some difficult days and nights. I'm thankful for all officers from across the state for working along with my security.

I'll never forget the law enforcement officers who stood behind me the day I signed SB 1070. Thanks to the Arizona Police Association, the Phoenix Law Enforcement Association, the Fraternal Order of Police, the Maricopa County Sheriff's Office and all of the other law enforcement organizations and officers who have supported me and the rule of law.

I appreciate Director Gilbert Orrantia of the Arizona Department of Homeland Security and his service to our state. I especially want to recognize the men and women of the Arizona National Guard and Major General Hugo Salazar, who serve and protect us.

Numerous others helped me fight the battles. Grant Woods, whom I've admired for years, thank you for keeping me balanced and always sharing the other side of the story. To Mary Peters, I appreciate that you're a feisty fighter who also tells it like it is and can fearlessly deliver a message. Your phone messages always made me feel better!

I'm thankful for Chuck Coughlin and Doug Cole, who have been my friends and advisers during the best of times and during the difficult times. Thanks to Paul, Ryan, Kate, Megan, Steve, and Tim, for their creativity and dedication. I appreciate Jay Heiler, who always provided the right words for the right occasions, and Lisa Hauser for keeping all of us in line and for all of your hard work in so many aspects. We won't miss those Thursday meetings, but thanks to everyone else who faithfully attended, including Pat, Kelli, David, Max, and Sarah. There are so many people to thank and there isn't enough room to mention everyone, and I apologize for those who aren't listed.

A special thanks to Sue Krentz for her help and for her stark reminders that our border is not secure, regardless of what the federal government is telling us.

Finally, the prayers and encouragement from everyone at Life in Christ Lutheran Church have meant so much to me during these past couple of years. Words can't express how grateful I am to all of you.

My job would be impossible without all the support and encouragement from people all across the country. Thank you! You all know who you are!